Crafts, Customs and Legends of Wales

Crafts, Customs and Legends of Wales

Mary Corbett Harris

DAVID & CHARLES
Newton Abbot   London   North Pomfret (Vt)

British Library Cataloguing in Publication Data

Harris, Mary Corbett
   Crafts, customs and legends of Wales
   1. Handicraft — Wales — History
   2. Tales, Welsh   3. Legends, Welsh
   4. Wales — Social life and customs
   I. Title
680   TT63

ISBN 0-7153-7820-1

Printed in Great Britain
by Biddles Limited, Guildford, Surrey
for David & Charles (Publishers) Limited
Brunel House   Newton Abbot   Devon

Published in the United States of America
by David & Charles Inc
North Pomfret   Vermont 05053   USA

Contents

cures — phantom funerals — where no dog will go — strange beings that haunt water — marriages between fairies and mortals — a link with the Iron Age — origins of medicine in Wales — lake with two names and two personalities — legends of King Arthur and of the river Dee — sacred wells

Acknowledgements

Thanks are due to the Editor of *The Countryman* for permission to quote from two articles; the Curator of the Welsh Folk Museum, St Fagans, Cardiff, for permission to take various photographs in the museum; Mr Douglas Hague, for permission to quote from his article on Rug Chapel in *The Journal of the Merioneth Historical & Record Society;* Mr J. Geraint Jenkins, Welsh Folk Museum, St Fagans, Cardiff, for permission to quote from his book on tanning; Meredith & Sons, Dolgellau, Gwynedd, for information concerning their fellmongers' business; Lord and Lady Newborough, for permission to write an article on their privately owned Anglican chapel at Rug; Area Record Office, Penarlâg, Dolgellau, and the Archivist's Office for making available various documents.

Most of the prices quoted are in pounds, shillings and pence. One shilling (1s) is equivalent to five new pence (5p) and two old pence (2d) are approximately equivalent to one new penny. There are twelve old pence to one shilling and twenty shillings to one pound.

To Celia, in affectionate remembrance

1

Drovers and Hill Farms

From time immemorial until recent times, thousands of sheep and cattle were raised on the barren Welsh mountains and in the remote valleys. Indeed, in the old county of Merioneth, now part of the new county Gwynedd, the whole rural economy was based on the small hill farmer, who by dint of hard and ceaseless toil was able to support himself and his family.

Though it is impossible to say with any certainty when the cattle trade between Wales and England began, it is known to go back to the dim past, and there are numerous references to it in medieval times. As long ago as 1312 the Chamberlains of Carmarthen and North Wales were expected to provide 700 oxen for the King; in 1317 the Bishop of Winchester bought fat cattle for the household of the Chancery; in the fifteenth century English troops in France were partly provisioned by Welsh cattle, and Nicholas Harwode was commissioned in 1417 to buy cattle from various parts of Wales for the King's use. The peaceful conditions which prevailed between England and Wales under the Tudors did much to foster the trade and by the sixteenth century many of the great English households were having cattle sent to them from Wales. There is mention of 'great fat oxen' and '100 fat muttons' being sent to the Earl of Leicester at Kenilworth in Elizabethan times.

The Civil War nearly put an end to this flourishing trade. Some North-Welsh gentlemen sent a pathetic petition to King Charles telling him that the stoppage of their sale of cattle 'threatens them with miserable famine'. Archbishop Williams in 1644 complained that the sale of cattle had entirely stopped and he wrote to Prince Rupert 'petitioning for our Welsh Drover, the Spanish Fleet which brings us what little gold we have'. The Welsh cattle trade was indeed considered so important that on 1 July 1645 the House of Commons ordered 'that Mr Speaker shall have Power to grant Passes to such Persons as he shall think fit, that shall desire to trade for the buying of Cattle in Wales and to drive and bring them to London.'

By the eighteenth century the Welsh cattle trade had become an exceedingly flourishing industry. Thirteen thousand head of black cattle passed through Herefordshire every year on the way to south-east England; Thomas Pennant wrote of 3,000 cattle being sold annually from the Lleyn peninsula alone, and another eighteenth-century writer stated that 20,000 beasts were sent to England from Cardigan. The animals were mostly store cattle, lean creatures from six months to three years old which would be fattened on the best English pastures before being slaughtered.

The animals had to travel enormous distances. They came from all parts of Wales and were driven to fairs and markets in Northamptonshire and Leicestershire, to Barnet in Hertfordshire, Ashford in Kent, various towns such as Chelmsford, Braintree and Colchester in Essex, and to Smithfield. In London a very large proportion of the milk trade was in the hands of Welshmen. It was stated 'the carriage and delivery of milk was entirely in the hands of women, strapping country wenches, principally recruited from Wales. The cows were kept in hovels in or near London; in 1808 it was calculated that about 8,500 cows were kept in London and its vicinity, one cow keeper in Islington owning between 800 and 900 cows.' The normal distance for a drove of cattle to walk was fourteen to sixteen miles a day at two miles an hour. From the Welsh coast to Northamptonshire took fifteen to twenty days; to Essex, three to four weeks, but there were frequent stops for resting and feeding, great care being taken so that the cattle were in good condition when offered for sale. A friend has told me that many drovers, like her grandfather Robert Griffiths, would never drive animals on a Sunday; to use his own words, 'the head drover rode before the drove arranging for their comfort during the week-end and what was astonishing, the droves that were rested on a Sunday, took three days less to do the journey than the animals which had no rest.'

Droves from different areas often joined together at various recognised meeting places so by the time the English border was reached it was not uncommon to meet herds of 300 or 400 cattle. Cobbett says that in separate droves he met 2,000 Welsh cattle from Pembrokeshire between Cirencester and Cricklade going to fairs in Sussex. Many different routes were taken and wherever possible the turnpike roads were avoided, for the average toll of one shilling per beast could amount to a considerable sum as toll gates occurred all too often. The frequent hold-ups not only caused delays but upset the animals, making them restive and difficult to manage, so whenever possible, tracks well-known to the drovers were used instead. Often they were ancient drift-ways, defined in an old law book as 'common ways for driving cattle', and sometimes the beasts were driven along the crests of the hills by paths that dated from prehistoric times. Even today, memories of the drovers are preserved in such names as 'The Welsh Way' in Gloucestershire and 'The Welsh Ride', a grassy path between gorse and heather in Hampshire.

Besides tolls, the chief expenses on the journey were hay and grass for the animals, and food and lodging for the men. The senior men in charge of the herd paid 4d to 6d for a bed at an inn, but their helpers just slept under hedges in the fields with their beasts. The following extracts are from expense accounts for driving 58 beasts from mid-Wales to Chelmsford, in October 1841:

Boy drive the beasts	2	0
Newbridge on Wye tavern ale	6	(3d per pint)
Llandrindod Wells grass	13	6
Pay John at Radnor for shoeing	£1 1	0
Northampton tavern	18	0
Man mind beasts	1	6
Ongar grass	£1 2	6
Other expenses at fair and return journey	£1 18	0

Early in the nineteenth century drovers were paid 3s a day for driving cattle from Haverfordwest to Ashford in Kent, plus a 6s bonus on reaching their destination. They also supplemented their earnings by selling milk when near any sizeable town.

Before starting on their long trek to England the cattle had to be shod, a hazardous task for the smith, for the animals were wild and had to be thrown and tethered first. One man, the 'feller' or 'overthrower', threw a rope round the bullock's horns, his helper bent one of the animal's forelegs, the horns were twisted sharply and the beast fell to the ground. All four legs were bound and then securely tethered to a piece of iron about 3ft long, forked at one end, which had been firmly driven into the ground. While one smith trimmed the hoof, another smith nailed on the shoes. They were quite different from those used for horses, much thinner and lighter, and were made in two sections to fit neatly over the cloven hoof, so each bullock had to have eight shoes or *ciw* as they were called.

One well-known smith in Bala used to spend the winter months making hundreds of shoes in readiness for the exodus in spring and summer. Once he and three helpers had to shoe a large herd of cattle in a field which sloped down to the Wnion river just by Dolgellau bridge. The bullocks were large and more than usually refractory, and one, a huge beast from Anglesey, dragged the 'feller' and his assistants into the river, but it is recorded that the men triumphed in the end and 'that

12

Merioneth had Anglesey down on his back.' The rates for throwing and shoeing varied from 9d to 1s per beast, and near villages where fairs used to be held, *cae pedoli* or shoeing fields can often be found.

A distinctive feature of the droves was the tremendous noise they made. This came not only from the beasts themselves but also from the men in charge, who shouted and hallooed at the tops of their voices as the cavalcade moved slowly through the English countryside. This was done on purpose because the drovers' well-known cry of *'Haiptrw ho!'* warned farmers that a drove was approaching so they had time to get their own cattle out of the way, for once entangled with the drove it would be almost impossible to separate them.

Though nearly all the cattle from Wales went to England by road, there are records of their going from various ports in south Wales by sea to Somerset, and before the Menai Straits were bridged, the unfortunate animals from Anglesey had to swim to the mainland. Several nineteenth-century writers have given eye-witness accounts of herds of terrified cattle swimming the often turbulent waters. To save some in danger of being swept out to sea, men in boats would throw ropes round their horns and drag them to the shore. When they reached dry land some were too exhausted to stand, others were terrified and 'became more like wild than domesticated animals, the whole scene being one to make humanity shudder.'

The ordinary Welsh drovers, who have been called a 'pertinacious people', had little English — one of them is supposed to have said that 200 words were sufficient if business was good, but a few more were necessary if a hard bargain had to be driven. Opinions about them varied, but on the whole they were reliable men. Under the laws made during the reigns of Edward VI and Elizabeth I, all drovers had to be householders, married men of at least thirty years of age, and they were required to hold licences, issued annually by the

13

Quarter Sessions of the County in which they had lived for three years. These licences gave great protection to their holders, protecting them from being apprehended under a law against 'forestallers, regraters and ingressers', and also protecting them from being taken up as vagabonds, for a Tudor document states that 'most of those that walke about be Welchmen'.

As well as driving cattle, the drovers performed all kinds of useful social services. Roads as we know them were practically non-existent and few people took the hazardous journey from Wales to England if they could help it, but by the drovers it was possible to send letters and messages to London and to execute commissions. Many drovers during the reign of Charles I acted as government agents and brought Ship Money to London that they had collected in Wales; in Cromwellian times too drovers were used as tax collectors, and rents from estates in Wales were frequently transmitted to landowners living in London by the same means.

The drovers seldom took the money they were entrusted with to England for fear of being robbed on the way, but settled the various accounts with money obtained from the sale of their cattle. From this it was but a brief step to the establishment of private banks and early in the nineteenth century several banks in England and Wales were started by members of the droving fraternity. One of the best known was at Aberystwyth: the Bank of the Black Sheep had a black sheep engraved on its notes. These were issued for £1, £2 and upwards to £10, the number of sheep depicted corresponding to the number of pounds represented — useful for those who could not read. Another well-known bank was founded at Llandovery in 1799 by a drover, *Banc-yr-Eidion Ddu*, the Black Ox Bank, its notes engraved with a black ox.

By the 1870s the railways had practically replaced long-distance drovers, though some of them attended Bodmin fair in the 1870s, still dressed in their traditional broad-rimmed hats and coats of Cambrian 'freeze'. But within living memory, during a prolonged railway strike in 1912, once again, out of the mists and mountains of Wales, emerged the drover and his cattle. For the last time the English countryside was filled with the noise of ironshod cattle trudging along the roads, and the once-familiar cry *'Haiptrw ho!'* was heard in the land.

From very early times the rearing of cattle rather than crops has been the chief occupation of Welsh farmers. It was natural that in such a pastoral society cattle were valued and even venerated above all other animals, for on their well-being and fertility depended the prosperity of the whole community. This close link between the people and their cattle is reflected in Welsh folk tales and laws, and language for the everyday things of life. Some of the most ancient race memories and stories stretching back to pre-christian times are concerned with the *ychen banwy*, long-horned oxen of prodigious size, great creatures of power and mystery, dimly looming through the mists of time. One of these stories tells of the monster dwelling in Llyn Llion which terrified the people living nearby till it was pulled out of its watery home by the legendary hero Hu Gadarn and a large team of *ychen banwy*, dragged up a pass — still called *Bwlch-Rhiw-yr-Ychen*, the Pass of the Slope of the Oxen — and finally killed. There are a number of very ancient stories about fairy cattle, *Gwartheg-y-llyn*, Kine of the Lake, being captured by mortals, serving them well for years, and then because of ill-treatment being called back to their fairy homes.

The men who first brought the Gospel to Wales were quick to appreciate the importance of cattle, and there are many legends linking the old Celtic saints with cows. St Brynach's very strange ménage, which consisted of a cow that was tended by a wolf, is remembered by several Welsh place names: *Cas Fuwch*, 'Cow's Castle' and *Castell Blaid*,

'Wolf's Castle' in Pembrokeshire, and Cowbridge in Glamorgan. St David had two famous oxen, and another holy man when he sailed across the Bristol Channel from Llantwit Major to Watchet took his cow as his sole companion and most precious possession. Long ago in Celtic lands milk was considered a sacred drink, so the early church, in the realistic way it often transformed pagan beliefs into Christian legends, tells of several saints like St Winifred, St Illtyd and St Llawddod who had magic wells that sometimes produced milk instead of water.

In the Welsh words for some of the everyday things in life one is reminded of cattle: the strong moisture-laden wind from the west — the prevailing one in Wales — is poetically called *Gwynt froen yr ych*, 'The Wind of the Ox's Nostrils'. The Celtic year began on 1 November; the Welsh name for the month is *Tachwedd,* literally 'the closing view', signifying that this was the time for slaughtering the cattle as there would no longer be sufficient pasture to feed them. In North Wales even today, November still holds special significance for the farmer and his stock, because it is then that the cattle leave the fields until about April, to be housed in barns of rough stones, with oak rafters and slate roofs, so strongly and skilfully constructed that many of them are still in use.

Up to the beginning of this century nearly all the cattle in North Wales, Cardigan and Pembrokeshire were the *Gwartheg Duon Cymreig,* Welsh Blacks, the native cattle of Wales and one of the very oldest breeds in Great Britain. No wonder Welsh farmers are proud of their cattle, for having for many centuries been bred and reared on bleak mountain farms they have inherited a famous toughness and longevity. They give excellent milk with a high percentage of butterfat and then end up as first-class butchers' meat. A writer in 1838 said of them, 'they thrive in every situation. They will live where others starve and they will rapidly outstrip most others when they have good pastures.'

16

Due largely to the fact that the Welsh-speaking farmers often lived in inaccessible hill farms, their cattle did not become well-known until after World War II, but now demand for them is growing. The breed is being built up abroad and a number can even be found in the Falkland Isles, where they do well, though the climate tends to be wet and cold. Welsh Blacks are now often crossed with Herefords.

After World War II, the age-old pattern of life changed. A vital part of the farms were the mountain sheep-walks where the sheep grazed during summer, so when thousands of these acres were planted with conifers by the Forestry Commission, many small farms became no longer viable and were given up. Also, numbers of men, specially the younger ones, felt that the old way of life was too hard, and, attracted by the higher wages obtainable elsewhere, left the land forever.

There are, however, just a few men like Lewis Williams for whom the way of life remains more important than money. His roots are too deeply embedded in the soil of Merioneth for him ever to leave it; his whole life has been spent at Tyddyn-bach where his family have farmed for five generations. Highly as he values the old way of life, there is nothing old-fashioned in the way he runs his farm, which with its modern machinery and milking parlour, sheep and pedigree cattle, can more than hold its own in the competitive world of modern farming.

The slate-roofed, 200-year-old stone house with its 4ft thick walls lies almost at the end of a lonely, fertile valley where strangers seldom penetrate. The farm consists of 155 acres of rough land, 65 acres of leys, of which about 20 acres are used for growing hay for the cattle, and approximately 1,000 acres of mountain sheep-walk. Of the 270 breeding ewes, most are pure Welsh mountain sheep, extremely attractive animals with their startlingly white fleeces and long tails which are never cut; they are exceptionally good mothers and very sturdy. It has been said of them that they are 'a breed so hardy that they can be raised in situations where no other animals could live.' They need to be tough, for the ewes always lamb in the open, however severe the weather, though if necessary motherless lambs are hand-fed at the farm until strong enough to fend for themselves; one lamb, born during a wet night, found sodden, weak and wretched, was saved by being taken into a warm kitchen and thoroughly dried with an electric hair-dryer.

Lewis Williams has five rams, putting the best of his ewes to his pure-bred Welsh rams and the less good to the Suffolks. In the spring the sheep are given swedes, sugarbeet and nuts, but Welsh mountain ewes are small, so if they have been put to large Suffolk rams, great care has to be taken with their feeding during the last six weeks of pregnancy. By this time the lamb has grown quite large, and the ewe cannot consume too much bulky food, so concentrates are given instead, and not too much, or the lamb will be too big and the birth difficult. During lambing, Lewis Williams is constantly inspecting his ewes. One afternoon this spring I was walking round the fields with him and his 15-year-old daughter, Anne, when they spotted a ewe in trouble, unable to give birth to her lamb as one of the forelegs was in the wrong position. With some difficulty she was caught, — very quickly the lamb was turned and delivered. A few seconds after its birth, the ewe was contentedly licking it all over and soon suckling it.

Lewis Williams comes from a line of successful stockmen. His great-great-grandfather was well known over a wide area for the way he could cure sick animals, and throughout succeeding generations there has always been at least one member of the family with an almost magical power with sick animals. As a child I watched fascinated while Lewis Williams' great-uncle set the broken leg of a sheep with warm pitch. Though Welsh sheep are notoriously wild, I

18

remember her lying in the yard at Tyddyn-bach, perfectly quiet and obviously unafraid.

Lewis Williams starts breeding from his ewes when they are eighteen months old, their breeding life depending upon their quality — perhaps five to six years — but he has had fine lambs from 11-year-olds. The excessive maternal instinct of Welsh mountain ewes can occasionally be embarrassing, for one which has not yet had her lamb will sometimes try and appropriate another ewe's, and can cause so much trouble that she has to be penned by herself till she has lambed.

In North Wales at the end of April or the beginning of May — depending on the weather — the sheep and lambs go to the mountain sheep-walks. Though a number of farmers may send their sheep to the same mountain, territorial instinct is so strong that the animals keep to their own part of the mountain — to their *cynefin* as it is called. So strong is this instinct that when a farm is sold the sheep are sold with it, for if moved they would not settle. Tyddyn-bach is surrounded by mountains and on one, round which winds the famous Precipice Walk, is a sheep-walk belonging exclusively to the farm. Further away, on Rhobell, a mountain stretching up for nearly 2,000ft, Lewis has another sheep-walk which he shares with a number of other farmers.

In August the flocks leave the mountains, and though Lewis sells a number of lambs, some are kept to replace the older sheep that are also sent to the fairs. During the severest winter months the remaining lambs are sent to Arthog, a few miles nearer the coast where the climate is much milder. I can remember when the charge for each sheep for the winter was 3s to 3s 6d; last winter Lewis paid £2.50 a head. In the old days, after shearing, the farmers would sell their fleeces where they pleased, often having them woven into blankets or cloth for their own use. Now all wool has to be sent to the Wool Board.

There is a small but fine herd of pedigree cattle at Tyddyn-bach — Welsh Blacks — including a bull bred on the farm and also some Friesians. In Merioneth cattle are not kept in barns just across the farmyard, but in small stone buildings among the fields, often quite a long way from the house. Fodder is stored in lofts above the cattle, so carrying feeding stuffs presents no problems, and when spring comes the muck can be spread on the nearby land. The cattle are mostly kept in from October to April or May. Though recently the Tyddyn-bach animals have been wintering out-of-doors, their feed supplemented by hay, sugarbeet pulp and nuts, on the whole Lewis prefers the older method and intends to revert to it, manure being so valuable; also the 'poaching' of the fields in such a wet climate is a disadvantage. Lewis finds that his farm economy is best balanced by going in for both autumn and spring calves. Autumn calves bring the disadvantage that the cows have to be better fed all through the winter if they are suckling, but on the other hand these calves are much larger and therefore sell better at the end of the following summer than the spring calves which have cost less to rear. The cattle are tuberculin-tested and brucellosis-free, and for the last 18 years, whatever the weather, Lewis Williams's wife, Ceinwin, has delivered milk all around the little village. Having tiny hands and great skill she is specially helpful with the sheep and can often deliver a lamb when no one larger could do so. The three children also help on the farm. Anne seems to have inherited her mother's skill with sheep, Olga rides her pony round all the outlying fields every evening at lambing time, just before dusk, to report if anything is wrong, and her young brother is already becoming interested and involved with various jobs.

Though life is hard at Tyddyn-bach — harder than most people would care for — it would be difficult to find a happier couple than Lewis and Ceinwin Williams. In a way that few people achieve, they have the best of two worlds, material and non-material. Between them, they not only run a financially successful farm, but they are also leading the way of life they prefer above all others, far from the modern rat-race and close to the soil and to a world of older values.

Time softens the harsh outlines of days which have gone forever, so there is a tendency to think that the way of life on the old farms was almost perfect. Much was undoubtedly good, but even allowing for the difference in the real value of money, extracts from the notebook of a Merioneth farmer, Hugh Jones, show how hard people worked and how little they earned 130 years ago.

1844	Harris Jones, Gwyddelfyndd. A year's wage from Hugh Jones, Gelli, £7 5s 7d. From the Mistress,	2 6d
1845	May 14th, Hugh Jones Pays Sara Evans for a year's washing,	10s 7d
1845	May 16th, Hugh Jones bought two shirts from Miss Jones, The Shop, Dolgelley,	4s 6d
1845	June 13th, Hugh Jones bought a new broom,	8d
1845	September 26th, William Roland to Hugh Jones	
	Making trousers	2s
	Waistcoat	1s
	Legins	4s
1846	Refooting stockings (knitted)	8d

Gwyddelfynydd was a farm near the river Dysynni and one winter a bullock was drowned in it. But in those days of sparse living and stern economy, nothing was wasted, so the animal was cooked and the meat served to the servants. When they refused to eat it, another bullock was killed and the meat from both animals was mixed up so no one knew which he was eating.

In the old days, slaughtering was done at home, the carcase being cut up and sold to neighbours in quarters or half-quarters, which were salted down and hung from the rafters of the kitchen until required. When a fat cow of Hugh Jones's was killed on 1 February 1867, these prices were obtained:

Head 3s; tripe 1s 6d; tongue 2s 6d; liver 1s; fat 15s 4d;
skin, weighing 65lb at 2½d a lb, 13s 6d   £1 16 10

Sold	Mari Jones, Galltygarw, a quarter at 6½lb, weighing 124lbs	3	7 2
,,	quarter shoulder to Mam, 124lbs at 6¼lb	3	4 7
,,	a half quarter to Lowri Williams, Pwllgela, 61lbs at 6½	1	13 0
,,	the other half quarter to Mari Edwards, Bronfoel, 61lbs at 6½ lb	1	13 0
,,	Mari James, Tynewyd, half quarter, 59lbs at 6¼	1	10 8
,,	Iona Puw, Bryngoch, half quarter, 59lbs at 6¼	1	10 8

£14 18 0

A moving story lies behind the seemingly commonplace entry in Hugh Jones's notebook 'Pay Gwen Lloyd £4 5s'. When Gwen was six years old an illness left her paralyzed from the waist downwards. Yet she led a full and active life, becoming an expert needlewoman who went all over the district, visiting the various farms and sometimes staying for as long as a fortnight, sewing and dressmaking. She rode everywhere on a pony and as long as someone helped her to mount and dismount, she was able to manage. She also taught music, and did not die till 1924, aged well over seventy.

As life became a little less hard, the routine at Glasgoed, 900ft up in the mountains north of Dolgellau, can be taken as typical of that on small farms during World War I and in the 1920s. Excluding the sheep-walk of about 60 acres, shared with two other farmers, Glasgoed consisted of just over 12 acres. The Thomases had a flock of about 24 sheep, two or three cows, a couple of pigs and some 20 fowls. With a well-stocked vegetable garden sheltered by stone walls from the chill winds that swept up the valley, the family were largely self-supporting in food, and their blankets were made of wool from their own sheep. The situation was too bleak to grow much grain but there were four small hayfields. In the absence of a horse, the hay was carried on someone's back — it had to be roped in a special way — or a large haycock was placed between two poles and carefully conveyed to the loft above the cowshed.

Glasgoed was not large enough to support a growing family, but John Thomas was a hardworking, gifted man who could turn his hand to anything and could always find an additional job. At one time he worked in the slate quarries at Ffestiniog, and after that he was at the Gwynfynydd gold mine, walking there and back, many miles every day over the mountains by sheep tracks and footpaths. He had many adventures. Once when he was in charge of some blasting operations, he and another man were at the bottom of a deep shaft in Gwynfynydd mine. He sent his mate up the long ladder and having seen his safe arrival at the top, lit the fuse and hastily made for the ladder himself. But at that precise moment the ladder broke, cutting off his sole means of escape. With great presence of mind he dashed back to the fuse and was able to put it out before it ignited the dynamite. After the gold mine closed he had various other jobs and did not retire until he was seventy-two.

Like many other farmers' wives, Mrs Thomas brought up a large family successfully on a meagre weekly wage. There were no modern conveniences of any kind at Glasgoed; every drop of water had to be carried from a nearby spring, yet the house was spotlessly clean and immaculately tidy and Mrs Thomas always had leisure for a chat. Cooking for a large family on one open fire cannot have been easy but Mrs Thomas put a huge saucepan on the fire in which she placed the meat and vegetables, among which, a little later, the pudding in another receptacle was carefully placed. Thus two courses would both be ready at the same time. All the bread was baked in the bread oven, built in the thickness of the wall on one side of the huge fireplace.

Brwas made a filling and nourishing meal. Between layers of bread various fillings were put in, such as cheese, onions, or anything else that happened to be available; the whole mixture was then moistened with mutton broth. It was thoroughly heated over the fire and served piping hot when the hungry men came in from work. This was proper *brwas*, the kind that would be provided at Glasgoed, but there was also a poor kind only given by mean farmers to their servants. This consisted merely of bread and butter flavoured with salt and pepper and moistened with boiling water. It was contemptuously and aptly called *brwas pig tegell* — literally *brwas* 'from the kettle spout'.

Two pigs were generally kept at Glasgoed — in those days it was reckoned that one paid for the other. They roamed free most of the time and only towards the end of their lives were they fattened on something inexpensive like bran. No part of a pig was ever wasted; brawn was made from the head, faggots from the heart and liver, while Mrs Thomas made an excellent pudding from the blood which was mixed with a little oatmeal or rice, flavoured with an onion, and cooked very slowly. The trotters were another delicacy.

Once when I called at Glasgoed, Mrs Thomas was about to make oatcakes — or *bara ceirch*. I am glad I learned exactly how they were made, for only a very few people are now left who know the traditional way of making them, over a wood fire, and using an oatcake turner. First of all the open fire was well banked up with wood; apparently oatcakes do not taste as nice if baked over a coal fire. Lard and butter were mixed together in a large cup with a little warm water. The oatmeal and the fats were then rubbed together and rolled out on the kitchen table. Pastry-boards were never used in the old mountain farms, for the tables, nearly always made of pale sycamore wood, were scrubbed so often and so hard that they were always snowy white and felt soft to the touch, like velvet. When the oatmeal was rolled out really thin, Mrs Thomas cut it into a number of little rounds with the rim of a cup, and after testing that the bake-stone was hot enough she carefully placed the oatcakes on it. When cooked on one side, the oatcake turner was brought out. In the old days all the farms had them; they were generally made of oak or sycamore, of varying designs, and were proudly handed down from one generation to another.

Another treat at Glasgoed were 'light cakes', a kind of pikelet or crumpet, but buttermilk was used which made all the difference. They were cooked in a frying pan over the open fire and eaten straight away with perhaps a little butter or jam. There was no money for intoxicants at Glasgoed but Mrs Thomas made excellent ginger beer, thirst-quenching and palatable; also cheap.

As long as the Thomases lived at Glasgoed, one had but to open the little wooden gate under the ancient holly tree and lift the latch of the door — which was never locked — to find the warmest of welcomes in the large, stone-flagged, typical Welsh kitchen. It was a comfortable place, especially in the evenings when the curtains were drawn across the windows, the oil lamp lit and the firelight flickering on the glass-fronted cabinet filled with china; the grandfather clock, the hanging bookcase crammed with Welsh books, the chairs with their patchwork antimacassars, the brass warming-pan on the wall, the couch under one of the windows and the two tables made of sycamore. From the great beams across the ceiling hung home-cured sides of bacon; there were long nails where the hazel walking sticks with curved handles—*ffon gollen*—were hung when not in use, and also the best Sunday boots. On one side of the fireplace stood the chair in which John Thomas always sat, on the other side, a small oak settle. From the enormous chimney a chain, blackened by the wood smoke of countless years, held a large kettle, singing away, always ready to make a rich brew of tea.

This way of life continued unchanged until the last of the

25

Thomases left in 1955. Since then the old house has been empty, the hospitable door is locked, the hearth grown cold, and no smoke will ever again rise in a welcoming plume from the great chimney, for Glasgoed is now a ruin, like a number of other old cottages in the district.

In Merioneth fifty years ago there was hardly a farm or cottage dweller who did not keep a pig, but now, owing mainly to the high cost of feeding stuffs, there are few indeed and not often do luscious sides of bacon hang from the rafters in the kitchens. This is a real break with tradition, for from the earliest days pigs have played an important part in the Welsh economy. The tenth-century Welsh laws commonly attributed to Hywel Dda set out with meticulous care the precise worth of animals: third in importance came swine, only horses and cattle being considered more valuable. 'The worth of a pig, from the night it is farrowed until it dung, is one legal penny; whilst it suckles, which is three months, two legal pence, and thence onwards, until the swine go to the woods, it is a hog, and four legal pence is its worth.' The 'perks' which each member of the King's household might acquire were also carefully listed. Fifth in precedence was the Keeper of the Gateway and among his privileges was the right 'to have, of the swine, taken in pillage that pass through the gate, the sow which he shall be able, with one hand, to lift by her bristles until her feet are as high as his knees.'

Pigs are often mentioned in Welsh literature and folklore. One of the heroes in *The Mabinogion* is called Culhwch, because his mother wandering on a mountainside gave birth to him in a 'swine's burrow'. Also, according to the same source, the first pigs to appear in Wales were a present from Arawn, King of the Underworld, to Pryderi. When Math heard of these 'beasts such as were never known in this island before — small animals whose flesh is better than that of the flesh of oxen' he was anxious to obtain some, and after much difficulty returned triumphantly to Gwynedd from Dyfed with several.

The Celtic year began on 1 November. The preceding night was known as *Nos Calan Gaeaf* — the night before the winter. Well within living memory in country districts huge bonfires were lighted — *coelcerthi* — and so long as they blazed people gathered round, dancing and playing games. But when the flames died down there would be a hurried scramble home for fear the dreaded *Hwch Ddu Gwta*, 'the black sow without a tail', would catch the laggards. The following is a translation of one of the typical songs chanted in many parts of Wales:

> Home, home, let each try to be first,
> And may the Tailless Sow take the hindermost.

Pigs must surely be the only animals to have a saint's day named after them. Long ago it was customary for herds of swine to be turned into the oakwoods to feed off the acorns, on an appointed day, 24 June, the festival of St John the Baptist. In Wales it was called *Gwyl Ieuan y Moch* — The Festival of St John of the Pigs. I can well remember, about fifty years ago, watching herds of small black pigs happily rooting for acorns in an oak wood.

Young pigs were sometimes called 'carters' because they would be taken to market in carts, covered with coarse netting, but I remember a farmer who thought nothing of buying a young pig at Dolgellau Fair and carrying it on his back in a sack to his farm about six miles distant. But his father was more particular; no Dolgellau piglet was good enough for him. He had to get his from Bala, and carried it home some 15 miles over the mountains along rough tracks.

2

Animals — Practicality and Sentiment

Years before there were trained veterinary surgeons, every farmer had to know how to deal with illnesses and accidents among his stock. Some of the customs practised were strange, but often they were effective. Hywel Pugh, who was born in 1766, lived in such an isolated cottage, some miles north of Dolgellau, that even today there is no proper road up to it; yet he was well known over a wide area for his skill with farm animals, people coming from far and near to consult him. The epitaph on his gravestone in the windswept mountain churchyard of Llanfachreth, where he was buried in 1851, records that his ability and kindness were appreciated: 'Appeals for help to attend sick animals brought many people to Hywel Pugh. He nursed and gave such help as was needed to hundreds, nay to thousands of sick animals.' He died in 1910 and numbers of his descendants still farm in the district, many of them having a gift for dealing with sick animals.

His grandson, another Hywel Pugh, went to school in Shrewsbury, but plans for his further education were cut short by his father's sudden death; he had to return home and run the family farm. He undoubtedly inherited his grandfather's skill with sick animals, and he was a well-known figure riding for miles on his small Welsh pony, however bad the weather, along lonely tracks over the mountains to some isolated farm where there was trouble with the stock. An old book of his gives the ingredients and detailed instructions how to make up a great number of medicines, either to keep the stock in good condition or to relieve them when ill. Going to the chemist in the nearest town might mean a walk of ten miles there and back, so the medicines were mostly made from plants growing locally such as plantain, marshmallow, elderberries and valerian, called all-heal plant, to mention only a few, or from ingredients most housewives kept. For quinsy, a handful of *march fiere,* the common dog-rose, was boiled in vinegar, squeezed through a cloth, and then sweetened with honey or brown sugar. If a six-weeks-old calf was constipated it would be given a potion by placing 3oz of glauber salts, ½oz of powdered ginger and ½oz of fresh aniseed into a pan of boiling water, warmed to blood heat, and then when cooled given to the calf.

On the hill farms in the autumn when the lambs were moved from the mountain sheep walks, to the richer pastures in the valleys, they sometimes ate too much and got fat too quickly; their blood became out of order, as the farmers said. So 4oz mastic, 4oz red Sanders and 2oz of sassafras were all ground to powder and with 2oz antimony were tied in a cloth and boiled in 4 quarts of well-water till reduced to 2quarts, cooled and bottled. The lambs were brought in for the night and next morning each was given three spoonfuls of the mixture. The treatment had to be repeated every day for three weeks, otherwise it would be useless.

When a farmer wished to fatten a cow for the butcher, it was essential to dry up the milk and also to ensure that no sores developed on the udders. In the old days it was considered that the best time to do this was in the spring when the grass was dry. A mixture of 2oz bole armenic, and 6-8oz roach alum was placed in 1½ pints of boiling beer. A pint of good vinegar was stirred in and when the mixture was at blood heat it was given to the cow, which was then milked thoroughly, but not turned out into the fields until two hours later. The treatment was repeated in four days if the udders seemed sore. This was usually sufficient, though occasionally a third dose was required.

No animal taked kindly to being drenched (dosed), but a most ingenious method was evolved. The medicine was put into a cow's horn. This was held firmly in the middle with both hands, and the contents poured very slowly, to avoid choking, into the animal's mouth, which was held open by a helper. A drenching horn I have seen used is well over a hundred years old and was in use up to quite recent times. Pigs are extremely difficult to control, and the best way to drench one was to use an old boot with a hole cut in the toe, about the size of a shilling. The medicine was poured into the boot and the toe was pushed into the pig's mouth; the angrier he got, the more he sucked at the contents of the boot.

In the days before x-rays and the numerous clinical tests now available for early and accurate diagnosis by experts, farmers had to develop their own judgement and powers of observation. Some of them seemed to have had a kind of instinct or sixth sense for diagnoses.

Sometimes one sees a sheep or a cow endlessly turning round and round in a small circle — a horrible sight, for death is certain unless an operation can be performed. In Wales the disease is called *y bendro* — literally translated 'the bends'; it is caused by a watery cyst on the brain, sometimes as large as a goose egg, probably the result of the animal having had a blow from a fall or from fighting. It was thought too that it could be caused in a sheep if it grazes too much wet grass, or in cattle if they ate hay on which dogs had urinated.

Before the operation the exact position of the cyst was located by closely observing the animal's behaviour. If the head was held straight down, the cyst was on the bone in the middle of the forehead, and if the head was raised and held straight, the cyst was on the bone at the back of the skull. But if the head was held lopsidedly, one eye protruding more than the other, the cyst was just above it. The complete description in Hywel Pugh's book is too gruesome to give in full. Suffice it to say that the animal was felled, its legs securely roped and 'a strong man held the head in a position convenient for the operator'. Two 3in cuts in the form of a cross were made, the skin carefully folded back and secured. Then with a special instrument a circle of bone was cut out, when the cyst would spring up and could easily be removed. The circle of bone was carefully replaced, the skin folded back and the wound bandaged. Only a few months ago I was talking to an elderly farmer who told me he could well remember seeing this operation being performed on a sheep about thirty or forty years ago by a man who, though not a trained veterinary surgeon, used modern instruments and was most successful.

Perhaps it is the sentimental strain in many Welsh people which accounts for the fairly widespread custom of erecting memorials to pets, not only on privately owned land but also on consecrated ground. Near Bala stands the mansion of Rhiwlas, which for hundreds of years has been the home of the Price family, and in the extensive grounds there is a dogs' cemetery still in use. This was started many years ago by Richard John Lloyd Price, a well-known character and a great sportsman — it was at Rhiwlas that the first sheep-dog trials were held, over a hundred years ago. Mr Price had such a passion for dogs — at one time he kept 100 at Rhiwlas — that even in death he did not want them forgotten, so he set aside part of his grounds where his greatest favourites could be buried. Some of the inscriptions on the headstones are interesting. 'One Playful Dog. Faithful. Funny Fatpaws.'; 'Gather, age 17 years, 1886. Respected by all. Lovely by name. Lovely by Nature.' More sadly, 'Here lies Comedy, the best loved and dearest of all retrievers. Accidentally shot by her devoted and heart broken master, Octo. 2., 1877.'

Pets and working dogs belonging to the Price family and their employees are still buried in this cemetery — the ground is known as South America because there was once a gardener at Rhiwlas called Dai Edwards, who when asked to clear away the undergrowth from the cemetery, said, 'It's like a bloody South American jungle in there.'

R. J. Lloyd Price was one of those great eccentrics who flourished during the Victorian era. At one time he was in such financial straits that he put practically all his available money on a horse called Bendigo, which won its race, thus bringing him a very large sum of money. Part of this he spent on building a fine family vault in Llanfor churchyard, near Bala Lake. In gratitude to Bendigo, these words are inscribed above the massive oak door leading to the vault:

> As to the latter end I go
> To see my Jubilee,
> I bless the good horse Bendigo
> Who built this tomb for me.

Engraved on the stone on Bendigo's grave in Leicestershire is a list of the races he won and the words 'Bendigo was buried here, 1904.' He has been described by a man who knew him well as 'little black horse that died before breakfast'.

Some miles from Bala, the main road to Dolgellau climbs laboriously up the steep slope of Garneddwen which forms a watershed between the Dee and the Wnion rivers. It is wild, uninhabited country but, strange to say, on the lower slopes of the grim, treeless Aran which stretches up for nearly 3,000ft, is a modern animal cemetery, known as St Francis of Assisi's Garden of Rest. Planning permission was given and in 1968 it started off well. When passing soon after a 'funeral' one could see flowers laid on the grave. But now it has a neglected look. I was surprised to find how old some of the inscriptions on the headstones were: 'Vic had a Fit, died quick, 15 November, 1885'; 'Mrs Elisabeth Pawser. The Old Dame, May 1891-1905'. These came from a much older burial ground. 'Morgan, slow mover Run over' is explicit enough, and some are pathetic: 'To a little Dog, too much loved' and 'A

Welsh Pony a faithful friend for 32 years'. This reminds me of another horse who, like Bendigo, has a memorial in consecrated ground. In a lonely churchyard on a simple headstone are the dates of a child's birth and death, and her name. Below is an inverted horseshoe and the words 'Hester, her beloved companion'.

But no sentimental feelings are extended towards the predators that attack farm animals. As Welsh mountain ewes always lamb in the open, however vigilant the farmer, foxes are an ever-present menace. They tend to be on the increase, for not only can they find refuge among the lofty rocky mountains that surround the small hill farms, but also in the increasing acreage of the Forestry Commission's plantations. During recent years the remote parish of Llanfachreth, near Dolgellau, was particularly troubled by foxes, for hunting as understood in England was impossible and neither shooting nor trapping was effective enough.

Young Mr Iorweth Jones, a Forestry worker, set himself to solve the problem. He lives in a lonely stone cottage, which can only be reached by footpaths or by an unmade road winding through trees. On one side of this is a plantation of larches, on the other, one of those rather mysterious woods, undisturbed for over a century, where carpets of moss hang from the surrounding stone walls and the oak trees are festooned with ferns and lichens, to which few people ever come.

Though Mr Jones had always been deeply interested in hounds, he knew nothing about the skills of hunting. However, he studied the subject carefully, got advice from a number of experts, and some seven years ago he bought five foxhounds. His only helper is his wife and he now owns a flourishing pack of ten couples called the Llanfachreth Hounds, which hunt north Merioneth and part of Caernarvonshire very successfully, accounting for about 20 foxes each season. Every Saturday from the beginning of October until about the middle of March, Mr Jones sets off with a vanload of hounds — generally the whole pack. Because of the rocky crevices and awkwardly situated earths, the terrier which always accompanies him is more important than in most hunts.

The Meets are not advertised in any way, for in rural Wales news is disseminated by word of mouth as effectively as tomtoms were used in darkest Africa, and between 30 and 40 followers turn out each week. The hunt is deservedly popular for not only does it provide good sport but in such a lonely district it fulfils a social need, and the excitement which greets the arrival of hounds at an isolated hill farm can well be imagined.

The terrain is very mixed. When drawing the Forestry Plantations, where by far the greatest number of foxes are found, hounds drive them out to the waiting guns. But often the Llanfachreth pack hunts over the mountains and this is harder. Sometimes they search for their quarry above the well-known Precipice Walk, occasionally on *Moel Offrwm*, the Hill of Sacrifice, down whose precipitous slopes, according to tradition, human victims were thrown to appease the wrath of some now long-forgotten god. At other times they cross the treeless wastes of Rhobell which rises for over 2,000ft. In such wild country success depends to a great extent on the ability of hounds to hunt by themselves for a good deal of the time, yet up to now not one hound has been lost.

Some days there are Meets at Bontddu in the Mawddach Estuary, or at Blaenau Ffestiniog which is slate-quarrying country, or among less difficult terrain in the lovely vale of Maentwrog, or as far afield as Portmeirion in Caernarvonshire. Mr Jones has also hunted over the moors not far from the nuclear power station at Trawsfynydd. Until a short while ago these treeless moors which stretch for miles had been used by the Army as a firing range. But recently the Forestry Commission have been planting trees over a small part of them and now foxes have started to breed in the trenches between the young trees, dug for draining purposes. Hunting ends around 3 o'clock in the afternoon, by which time great distances have often been covered.

The majority of the hounds are Welsh, but some are English, and Mr Jones finds it perfectly easy to hunt both breeds together. The three Welsh hounds he is holding *(see page 101)* have long, hairy coats, whitish-grey in colour; the hound nearest the camera has brown markings; the other two have a streak of reddish-brown hair down their backs. The origins of Welsh hounds are a little obscure, but it is known that monasteries had special dogs to protect their flocks and that the monks at Margam Abbey in Glamorganshire had *'chiens fauvres des Bretagne'* imported from France during Tudor times. After the monastery was dissolved the monks gave their hounds to Sir Thomas Mansell who had become the Lord of the Manor of Margam, and later they went to a Mr Jones of Gelli, where the breed remained up to the twentieth century.

In the mid-eighteenth century, Hugh Vaughan of Hengwrt near Dolgellau kept a pack of foxhounds, but after they were dispersed in 1778, 'no other Squire took his place, and the foxes were left in peace or killed at will by the tenantry.' There are references to fox hunting round Corwen, Merioneth, in the 1860s, and during the period between the two world wars, occasionally hounds from mid-Wales were brought to Llanfachreth when the fox menace was acute. Today the Ynysfor, founded about 200 years ago, hunt on foot in other parts of Gwynedd. It is said that 'the Welsh hound has a great voice and it is truly a gratifying sight to a houndsman to observe them persevering in working out a cold scent through a flock of sheep.' Their powers of scent are said to be remarkable and their natures affectionate.

The cost of keeping the pack is great but fortunately Mr Jones gets financial help from various sources. The Forestry Commission gave a fox-destruction grant towards the hunt;

there is also a government bounty of £1.75 for each brush, and for some hunts a set fee is paid by the parish within whose boundaries a kill has been made. In Llanfachreth, however, for each fox destroyed within the parish boundaries, payment is made from the Llanfachreth Fox Destruction Fund, to which in theory all the farmers pay a *per capita* fee for each sheep they own; in practice, some pay more, others less. This money also goes towards the upkeep of the hounds.

The menace of foxes is nothing new. In pre-newspaper days, on Sundays after Matins, the bell ringer would stand on a mounting block outside Llanfachreth Church to make important announcements, among which very often were 'the rates to be contributed towards destruction of foxes'.

3

Crafts and Skills Now Gone

The little cottages in North Wales were strongly built of local stones and roofed with slates; they had to be well constructed for many of them clung precariously to the bleak mountainsides, shielded from the full force of the winds which swept up the valleys only by a few sycamores or some ancient, twisted damson trees. The fact that many of these old cottages have withstood the winds and rains for over 200 years is a great tribute to the skill of the craftsmen who built them, and in some measure must be due to the kind of mortar which was used. It was practically indestructible. When a friend of mine blew up a very old chimney, which once served an abandoned mine, it was blown from its foundations but fell to the ground all in one piece; even dynamite could not loosen the mortar. No one knows quite how it was made, but some of the ingredients were river sand, burnt lime, bullocks' blood and cattle dung.

The slate roofs of these cottages were also constructed in a way that is now obsolete; that is, with slates of different sizes, large ones at the bottom, ever smaller and smaller ones towards the top.

There are quiet hills and hidden valleys in North Wales so remote that even in high summer it is possible to walk for hours and never hear a sound except the sinister cry of the carrion crow and the roar of the streams as they cascade down the hillsides. Occasionally the traveller will come across small, grey-stone cottages where the old farm implements in the out-houses and the collectors' pieces still used every day in the kitchens give the impression that time has stood still.

One of the most unusual bygones is a *stric*, a four-sided wooden implement about 15in long with a round handle, which has been used from time immemorial for sharpening scythes. Two bullock horns were strung together by a piece of cord and slung round the farmer's neck. One horn contained grit. At the top there was a close-fitting wooden lid with a small hole, stopped with a peg. This could easily be pulled out when some grit was required. The other horn had its tip cut off for it contained lumps of *bloneg* — pig's fat — which would smell extremely pungently in warm weather if it had no ventilation. When the farmer wished to sharpen his scythe, he took some grit on to a piece of cloth — generally flannel — and rubbed it on the *stric* which he had previously greased with *bloneg*. The grit adhered and sharpened the scythe so effectively that even today there are still men who prefer this method to modern sharpeners. When he sharpened his scythe, a man balanced it over his shoulder, but great care had to be exercised, for his throat could easily be severed if the blade turned.

On old scythes there was a special peg on which to hang the *stric* and the initials of the owner were branded on the horn, so that at harvest time when a good many might be lying together in a field, no dispute about ownership could arise.

Sometimes on old oak dressers, among the china rolling-pins, china dogs, lustre jugs and Staffordshire figures, a large, yellowish-white shell may still be seen. It has a hole bored into it banded with metal. Fifty years ago, few farm workers could afford the luxury of a watch, so to call men in the distant fields back home for a meal, the farmer's wife would stand outside the house and blow through the shell, or horn as it was called, making a loud, wailing note which could be heard a great way off. One of my earliest recollections was the eerie note from one of these horns — some had been brought back from Patagonia — but they all produced a slightly different note so that there was no confusion.

Another curious bygone which I remember is a wooden

instrument called a *fleam*. It is rather like a large penknife but when opened, instead of blades four metal bars of different sizes appear, all sharply notched at the top. It could be used on humans or animals for blood-letting. A tourniquet was bound round a limb, the pointed end of the metal bar placed on an artery and smartly tapped with a mallet and the blood gushed out, to be controlled by the tourniquet. Pitch or tar was used to seal the tiny wound.

This particular *fleam* had been used for many years by the local blacksmith for it was considered beneficial for horses to have their blood let occasionally, and blacksmiths, always important people in a rural community, were often consulted as veterinary surgeons as well as doctors. During the acute depression of the mid-nineteenth century, when people were almost starving, a *fleam* might be used to draw off some blood from a cow; this was mixed with meal and made a blood pudding which satisfied the pangs of hunger for a time.

An old friend who died in 1964, age eighty-nine, was very proud of the sycamore rolling-pin which had been made for her as a wedding present. She also valued highly her polishing iron, which has a rounded rather than a flat base. She told me she used to flake up soap very finely, pour boiling water on it and then add a little turpentine. When this mixture had set into a jelly it was smoothed on to the collars of the shirts. Then the polishing iron was used and a wonderful gloss resulted.

In an isolated cottage a friend has a magnificent oak dresser made by her grandfather, as was the corner cupboard which would adorn any antique furniture shop. Hanging on a wall is a very strange barometer. It is a stiff card and attached to it in the centre are two ears of *yd ffrainc* — French oats — which move according to the weather: to the right for fair, to the left for rain, sticking straight out if no immediate change is coming. This simple gadget is known to be well over one hundred years old and still works perfectly. My friend used to bake all her bread in a traditional-style bread oven. Lined with bricks it was built into the thickness of the immense stone walls on one side of the cavernous fireplace. The oven was filled with lighted sticks; at first the bricks went black with heat, they then gradually turned white, and then the hot ashes were raked out and the big tins of bread put in quickly; perhaps a rice pudding as well. The bread took about two hours to bake but the rice pudding would be left in all night.

In some old cottages, rushlight candle holders may still be seen. At home we used wax candles and oil lamps but in some of the farms the *cannwyll frwyn* — rushlight candle — was in use. The late autumn was the best time for gathering rushes; the largest ones, growing in the wettest places, made the best candles for as they did not snap so easily they lasted longer. Very carefully the green outer covering was peeled off, except for a narrow strip which was left to strengthen the candle. Fat that contained no salt — this was essential — was heated in a metal pot with a long handle. The peeled rushes were drawn through the fat, and having been put to drip in another pot with a long handle, they were then drawn through the fat again; the number of times this was done depended on the size of the rush.

Though electricity came to North Wales in the 1960s, I knew one old lady who so much preferred the old way of lighting that she made and used rushlight candles until she died in 1967. She has told me that years ago numbers of people would go off to marshy ground and gather enormous quantities of rushes, tying them together in great bundles. Friends would meet together in one of the farms for what was called a *pil nos* — rush-peeling evening — and while some worked at the long and tedious job, others entertained them by playing the harp and singing or telling stories. Rushlights are 12 to 14in long, and the time they take to burn depends on their size; but on average, they would last not more than 20 minutes.

In the quiet uplands of North Merioneth, up to the 1920s,

one of the great events of the autumn was the advent of the *dyrnwr mawr,* the threshing machine, known as *injan Dafyd Jones,* because it belonged to a farmer of that name, and one of my greatest joys was to watch it working and follow it round from farm to farm. The harvest was late in the mountains because of the wet, cold climate, so threshing did not begin until the end of September or the beginning of October. Then one day we would see across the valley a plume of smoke rising near a large stone barn, and the still autumn air was filled with a rhythmic, humming noise, like the purring of a gigantic cat.

There were three machines — the one which did the actual threshing, the *malwr* or chaff-cutter which cut the straw into chaff when the grain had been extracted, and *y boiler,* the coal-fired engine that supplied the power for the machines. It looked rather like the earliest kind of steam engine, with a very long funnel topped with a metal crown which was supposed to disseminate the sparks and so lessen the risk of setting the ricks alight. The engine consumed an enormous amount of fuel — at one farm where only peat was burned the farmer had to order 15cwt of coal specially for threshing. From a large wheel on one side of the engine a wide belt ran to a smaller wheel on the threshing machine. Above the fire box was a water compartment and a water gauge that had to be watched carefully: a piece of lead floated in it, which if the water fell below the safety level, 'melted and put out the fire', thus preventing the boiler from exploding.

The threshing machine was a massive wood structure and the number of revolutions at which it worked, depending on the condition of the grain, was a vital matter decided by the threshing master. Oats were fairly easy to deal with if not mouldy or over-heated. Pitchforked in at one end, they were fed into a rotary drum, running at high speed, adjusted according to the condition of the grain. By complicated machinery the grain was separated from the straw and fed into a large riddle, and then into a cleansing rotary pan; lastly into a cleansing screen where it was sorted into first, second and third class and tailings. Then it poured like a stream into wide-mouth sacks. Barley had to pass through a 'huller' that removed the coarse hair guarding the grain. A special kind of barley with extra coarse hair was grown near woods to deter attacks by birds.

The setting up or *gosodiad* of the *dyrnwr mawr* was not easy, for it had to stand perfectly level, its wheels firmly scotched with stones to prevent it moving. At the turn of the century, Dafydd Jones charged 17s 6d for the setting up and the first four hours of threshing; 2s 6d for each subsequent hour. By about 1914, the respective charges went up to 27s 6d and 5s.

The scene by the big barn remains vividly in my memory: the cries of the men as they shouted instructions; the whirr and throb of the engine, every now and then belching forth clouds of smoke; the lean sheepdogs nosing around; the pale autumn sunshine touching everything with its beauty; and in the distance, wherever one looked, the majesty of the great mountains, keeping their eternal watch.

The machines were very heavy and cumbersome, so moving them from farm to farm along the narrow twisting lanes was a hazardous task. Some farms were up such steep cart tracks that as many as eleven straining, sweating horses, one in the shafts and five pairs abreast, would have to be used for the *dyrnwr mawr*, which was held with a number of ropes. Some farmers had no horses, none had more than two, so neighbours lent theirs, and it was quite a job sorting out the three teams. The rule was that the farmer whose grain was to be threshed was responsible for providing the horses. The *drynwr mawr*, or the 'box' as it was sometimes called, was the hardest to move; as it had no brakes, a piece of iron, called a 'shoe' for it was shaped like one, was used to help control the wheels down steep slopes. When manoeuvring and edging it through some specially awkward gateway, Dafydd Jones, its owner, would get agitated and hop about crying 'Mind the box *bach* — mind the box!' At the various farms enormous meals were provided for the workers — often beef, masses of vegetables and plum pudding — and there was friendly competition between the farmers' wives to provide the best food.

One lane was so narrow and had such awkward corners, that to avoid meeting a farm cart — motor cars were unknown — the machines were moved at night, a truly dramatic spectacle — the rattle of the iron wheels, the shouts of the men, the sparks struck by the horses' hooves from the stony road, and the fitful light of the candles in the lanterns bobbing up and down.

As it was impossible to haul *injan* Dafydd Jones up to Cwm, the most northerly part of the district, *injan* Robin-y-gof, a smaller machine belonging to a blacksmith of that name, visited the more inaccessible farms before World War I; the others had to thresh by flails. Children in the tiny school in that remote area were expected to help with the threshing, as well as the adults; an entry in the School Log Book, typical of many others, reads: '28th October, 1904, our attendance suffered badly, some of the children kept at home the last part of the week, owing to the Threshing Machine being in the neighbourhood.'

But farming in Cwm altered completely after compulsory ploughing orders were issued by the Government in 1917-18. For a couple of years the Ministry of Agriculture provided several small petrol-driven threshing machines, which after the war were sold to private individuals. They served a wide area until World War II, when compulsory ploughing was again introduced, and the Ministry of Agriculture provided much more up-to-date pneumatic-tyred machines moved by tractors. Some of the men who tended *injan* Dafydd Jones still speak of it with great affection; one of them indeed was so fond of it that he salvaged two of its wheels and now they lie in his front garden, filled with flowers.

The sound of threshing by flails was an unforgettable one which carried a long way in the quiet country air. Some sixty years ago, Dafydd Jones, who was a master of this difficult craft, would spend about two months at a farm each year. The sheaves were laid in two rows, about five or six in a row with the heads facing inwards, on a board made of oak or larch; there would be a man at each end of the rows beating in turn at a steady, rhythmic pace. The flail consisted of two pieces of wood a few inches wide. The head was about 2ft 6in long, the handle some 4ft long, and the two pieces of wood were joined together by a stout white thong, nailed to the top of the head and passed through a hole at the top of the handle. Great skill was needed to use a flail to the best advantage; it was no use hitting the sheaves with just the tip of the head — the art lay in rotating the handle rapidly in such a way that the whole length of the head was used for beating.

When the flailing was finished, the straw was carefully shaken lest any grain was left, and made into round bales, bound with a twisted strand. Then a machine winnowed the grain and also riddled it. At one farm, even higher up the mountain, the more old-fashioned method of winnowing by means of a blanket stretched on a kind of wooden frame was used. The frame was rotated rapidly by hand and the resultant current of air separated the grain from the chaff. But with this method the riddling still had to be done, with a pan, rather like a sieve for riddling cinders but square instead of round. This *gogr* needed great skill to operate, for it had to be shaken backwards and forwards in such a way that the grain went to the right side and the chaff to the left. I can remember other remote farms where the Biblical method of winnowing by means of a blanket shaken by hand was still used.

Finally the grain was taken to a mill, where it could be parched or baked so that it would keep dry during the long months until another harvest could be garnered. In the old days the miller did not receive a cash payment but he took what was called a 'toll' — that is, he was entitled to one scoopful from every sack of meal. The best oatmeal was kept in large oak chests or *cists*, and in order to store as much as possible, it was a common custom, even as late as the 1920s, for children, wearing specially knitted thick white stockings, to get into the *cists* and tread the oatmeal down, a job which they much enjoyed. Sometimes a little of the best oatmeal was fed to the pigs, in order to 'sweeten' the bacon, as the old country saying puts it.

Oatmeal was often used to make a cooling drink called 'shot', much enjoyed by thirsty workers in the harvest fields. A particular kind of oatcake was baked and then crushed with a piece of wood about 10in long, grooved in the middle with a handle at each end. Buttermilk was poured on the 'shot', the mixture was left to stand for a few hours and then it was carried out in large jugs, covered with a clean cloth, to the harvesters. A boy I knew was always getting in trouble for being late for school. One day he was particularly late and told the infuriated teacher, 'Please, I couldn't help being late, I was feeding *Taid* (Grandfather) with shot'. Being Welsh-speaking, the teacher fortunately knew what he meant.

The making of wooden soles for clogs is now a dying craft which was flourishing when I was a child. By the side of an old stone bridge was a grove of alder trees, and thither every spring came the clog makers; often the first sign of their presence was the blue smoke from the fires drifting about some nearby magnificent horse-chestnut trees. The alders were cut into lengths, which were in turn cut into small blocks, the right size for clogs. Then they were carefully shaped and trimmed, a skilled job, and finally stacked in large piles, several feet in circumference and height. It was a pleasant scene, a relic from a more peaceful age; the river flowing quietly by — in summer bright with mimulus — the blue smoke from the wood fires, the piles of newly made clogs, and the men busy with their ancient craft. They stayed a few weeks, then they would be gone as suddenly as they came, and the place knew them no more until the next spring. The clogs were sent away to have their leather uppers put on, and were sold in many of the Lancashire towns.

Another obsolete and highly skilled craft, before the advent of rotary saws, was the cutting of huge tree-trunks into planks with a cross-cut saw above a *pwll llif* — a saw pit. Among the last people to practise this skill were Robert Thomas and his two sons. It was essential that the planks were perfectly straight, so a rope was dipped in soot and stretched tightly along the tree trunk. When picked up and dropped, it flicked back into position leaving a straight black mark along which the Thomases could saw, Robert Thomas on top of the saw pit, his son below. It was an awkward job with long planks; cross-cut saws are not easy to manage, and on frosty days John Thomas would take off his boots to get a better grip when climbing in and out of the saw pit and walking along the tree trunks.

Few trees are now felled and processed for the tanning industry. 'Spring in the woods', or spring-*goed* to use the Welsh expression, sounds restful and romantic, but as late as the 1920s to many people in Merioneth the words conjured up long hours of hard and sometimes dangerous work. For spring, when the sap was rising, was the best time to fell the oak trees and strip off the bark to be used in the local tanneries in Dolgellau. At one time the little town was an important tanning centre, ideally situated to carry on this old industry. Hides and skins came from the hundreds of cattle and sheep raised on the nearby pastures and mountain sheep-walks; up to World War I nearly all the extensive woods in Merioneth were of oaks, and the two rivers, fed by many mountain streams, flowing through the town supplied the enormous amount of water required by a tannery.

Felling trees in the old days before mechanical aids were available was a lengthy and hazardous job. There was no lopping of the large branches and the crown of the tree as is done now, and I can remember how one end of a rope was attached to the top of a tree, several men pulling at the other end to ensure that the tree fell exactly in the required place. After the foresters, the spring-*goed* moved in; a photograph taken during the 1890s shows a group of men with the tools of their craft. A useful tool the men used constantly in the old days was a *pilbren,* the tool used for stripping off oak bark. It was roughly 3ft 2in wide and sharp-edged. The tree was scored about every 24in with a hatchet or bark knife, and vertical slits were then made. The next task of actually stripping off the bark was a very skilled one; the art lay in slipping the *pilbren* under the bark so as to bring it away in big, semi-cylindrical 'plates' — the larger the better for handling and loading on the carts which would transport them to the tannery.

The pieces of bark, anything from about 18in to 5 or 6ft long, had to be loaded with care, for the carts would have to travel a number of miles up and down steep hills along rough, twisting lanes to the tannery in Dolgellau. The largest pieces were put on the cart first in a criss-cross position, forming a kind of frame, and the shorter pieces were placed inside. The load was securely roped together and when at last all was ready and the cart rumbled off, it looked like a large log cabin moving along the road.

Tanning, the conversion of hides and skins into leather by steeping them in an infusion of astringent bark, usually that of oak trees, is one of the oldest crafts known to man. The skins had to go through a number of complicated processes. To make the tanning liquor, large dried 'plates' of bark were placed in the hopper of a water-driven grinding mill and pushed into rapidly revolving cutters. The finely ground bark was mixed with cold water in the 'leaching' pits and this liquid was next taken to the 'suspender' pits where tannage began. There might be as many as eight of these pits in a tannery. The hides or skins were suspended first in the pit (hence their name) holding the weakest solution and then by stages to the strongest. The hides had constantly to be moved and great care was taken that they did not touch, or they would colour unevenly. When they had passed through all the 'suspender' pits they went to the 'floater' pits, where they were placed flat; here quantities of ground bark were often added to the liquor to increase its strength. In the final set of pits, the 'layers', each hide was sprinkled with finely ground oak bark. This was the end of the actual tanning process, though of course much work still had to be done to the hides before they could be sold as leather.

Years ago, oak bark was used for another purpose as well. In the old days it was quite usual when someone was very ill to lay straw on the road outside the house to lessen the sound of passing wheels and horses' hooves. But in Merioneth, where owing to the heavy rainfall and lack of sun little grain was grown, straw was too precious a commodity. Oak bark was used instead in front of Dolgellau Assize Court when the Judge was presiding, and a friend of mine can remember this being done during the 1930s outside a house where a woman was dangerously ill, there being a great deal of traffic noise because of the nearby smithy.

In spite of the hard work, boys and men enjoyed the spring-*goed* but now this age-old craft belongs to the past like the woods of native oak in North Wales which have nearly all been felled. Any replanting is mostly with conifers.

Gold mining is another craft which has died out in Wales. The mines there have been derelict so long that few people remember that the red gold of Wales gave work to many, wealth to a few, provided the wedding rings for royalty and a magnificent regalia for a prince. It was once worked in various areas, principally near Dolgellau in Merioneth. Merioneth gold was probably mined from very early times, first by the Cymry, then by the Romans; while in the Charter granted by Prince Llywelyn in 1209 to the monks of the Cistercian abbey

(*above*) Bank note from the 'Bank of the Black Sheep', founded by drovers
(*below*) The cattle market at Llanwrst, about 1895

(*above*) An old print of Welsh countrywomen's dress. *Left to right:* farmer's daughters; farm servant; market woman; farmer's wife
(*below left*) Typical North Wales cottage
(*below right*) Hounds from the privately owned Llanfachreth pack, with their owner

near Dolgellau, it was specifically stated that among the many privileges were 'as a lasting gift . . . the right in digging out and carrying away metals and treasures in mountain and groves.'

In 1631 Thomas Bushel rented certain mines near Barmouth by royal warrant; four years later he was allowed to erect a mint at Aberystwyth castle by permission of Charles I. It is not known how many gold coins were minted, or how many are still in existence, but at the beginning of this century some were exhibited in Barmouth, among them a £5 gold piece showing Charles I, coined by Bushell in the Welsh Mint, with the Prince of Wales's plumes in place of the ordinary fleur-de-lys.

For the next two hundred years the history of Welsh gold mining is obscure, for though a local landowner granted leases for the prospecting and working of 'lead, copper or any other minerals' on some of his land as early as 1715 and 1724, gold does not seem to have been rediscovered until about 1834. Even then, apparently, no mines were actually opened for another ten years. However, by the middle of the century, gold was found in a series of quartz veins, some of which also carried quantities of silver, iron, copper and other metals, in the valley and estuary of the river Mawddach. This was known as the Dolgellau Gold Belt and twenty-four gold mines were operating in it at one time, the chief ones being at Gwynfynydd at the head of the Mawddach valley, a few miles north of Dolgellau, and at Clogau on the main road between Dolgellau and Barmouth.

It is around these two mines that the history of Mawddach gold mining revolves. The immemorial peace of the remote Welsh valley was broken. Miners came from many different parts, some from as far away as America, though the majority were local men. Some were accommodated in large barracks built by the gold mining companies, others walked long distances to and from their homes every day; some ran a little farm as well, for wages were not high. One man has told me

51

that as a boy his father worked a ten-hour shift for 6d a day.

Gwynfynydd was originally opened as a lead mine. Gold was discovered there in 1864 and in the 1880s was developed by that remarkable man Pritchard Morgan, known in Wales as the Gold King. He had been articled to a solicitor in Newport, but quarrelling with him one day he walked out of the office, straightaway sailed from there for Australia, started as a farm labourer, and within a few years became one of the richest farmers in the country. He continued his legal studies and became an eminent barrister, then turned his attention to exploring and gold prospecting and amassed a considerable fortune. But by the time he returned to England in 1884, he was almost ruined, for all his investments had gone wrong. He borrowed enough money to start prospecting for gold in North Wales, and soon felt certain he had discovered a rich vein at Gwynfynydd. Just in the nick of time his Australian investments recovered and he was able to lease the mine.

Enormous sums were spent on plant and machinery, a great deal of which came from Chicago, the Morgan Gold Mine Company was floated and on 18 July 1887 the miners struck a very rich vein of gold, at Number 1 level; it was so valuable that I have been told by a miner who was there at that dramatic moment that the two policemen regularly employed by the company were not considered enough to guard the treasure, and special police were drafted to the mine until the gold was extracted. By 31 May the next year, gold to the value of £14,000 had been extracted, only an earnest of the rich harvest to follow.

Among the 250 workers employed at that time was Hugh Pugh of Dolgellau. He lived to be a very old man and his diary, which he lent me, made fascinating reading.

> I started work at Gwynfynydd in 1888 and a lot of boys [with me] under 15. We used to meet on Dolgellau bridge at 3 o'clock [in the morning] with our Wallets, a big home-made loaf in one end and rations in the other and start work at 7 o'clock after

walking 8½ miles — no bicycles then. There was a gold rush here, miners everywhere and shops with trays of gold quartze selling to visitors going to Cader, Torrent Walk and Precipice. ...

At first the Clogau Mine was worked only for copper, but a rich gold vein was struck in 1860. At the Great Exhibition in 1862, the company that worked the mine was given a medal inscribed 'Medal awarded to the Vigra and Clogau Mining Company, for the first successful result in Britain, chiefly due to their Agent, John Parry, of a Gold-Bearing Vein.' During 1865 dividends were paid to the value of £22,575, and in just over three years gold was produced to the value of £42,783, the company receiving £3 18s for every ounce of gold obtained.

In 1891 four Barmouth people formed a company called the Clogau Gold Mining Company; this was taken over a few years later by another company, under the chairmanship of Godfrey Isaacs, brother of the first Marquess of Reading. In 1900 it was amalgamated with the Gwynfynydd Mine, under the name of St David's Gold and Copper Mines. Within the next twelve months about £60,000 worth of gold was extracted, and hopes ran very high that prosperity had come to this lonely, sparsely populated part of Wales. But gradually as the years passed, gold mining became less profitable, and even the amalgamation of Gwynfynydd and Clogau failed to save either. The story of gold mining in the Dolgellau Gold Belt virtually ended with the closure of Clogau in 1911 and Gwynfynydd some years later, though Clogau continued to be worked for a number of years by a couple of men.

The gold for Queen Mary's wedding ring and that of the late Princess Royal came from the old Clogau workings. It was from the Bwlchylli Mine, afterwards renamed the Prince Edward Mine, near Trawsfynydd, that sufficient gold was obtained, and presented as a gift to the Crown, to make the regalia for the Investiture of the Prince of Wales at Caernarvon on 13 July 1911. These beautiful items, a chaplet, verge, rings, sword and clasp, were designed by Sir William Goscombe John and are in the National Museum of Wales in Cardiff.

Glasdir, though a very small mine some four miles north of Dolgellau, where gold, silver and copper were mined, is of particular interest, for it was there that the Elmore oil flotation process for the extraction of gold was used successfully for the first time, and metallurgical and engineering specialists from all over the world came to see it. Glasdir closed down in 1914 and mining ceased officially in the Dolgellau Gold Belt, but unofficial working continued for a number of years.

One of the personalities in my village was Griffith Griffiths, a retired gold prospector. In the 1920s he could be seen wandering down a lane, past my home, ostensibly going for a gentle stroll, but in reality intent on business. Collecting two friends on the way, he walked up a lonely little valley to a desolate ravine through which a torrent thundered down in a silver cascade from the mountain top. High up beside the swirling waters were large holes, the entrances to a tiny gold mine which had been worked many years before and had actually been discovered by Griffith Griffiths. The ladders down the shafts had long since disintegrated but the old miner got his friends to lower him down on a rope into the mine, where he would remain for some time. When he was ready he signalled by tugging the rope that he wished to be drawn up, and he reappeared with a bag round his neck full of stones. At home, by means he never disclosed, he extracted the gold which he eventually sold, and it is said he made quite a good thing out of his unusual pastime.

As well as being a well-known and successful prospector for gold by orthodox means, he could find it by divining with a stick. But the mining experts who employed him refused to believe he had this gift, so he was taken up to London to the head office of the company, where some gold was well hidden in the board room. Holding a stick in his hand like a water diviner, Griffith Griffiths found it immediately. When he

died, the national press recorded that it was he who had pro-
cured the gold for the late Princess Royal's wedding ring.

There was certainly plenty of gold in Merioneth years ago
and sometimes it was put to strange uses. There was a very
popular tailor in Dolgellau, a convivial soul who liked to go on
a spree in the evenings with his many friends, but had a wife
who would go through his pockets, removing his money. He
got the better of her by using sovereigns as buttons on his suits,
covering them so neatly that his wife never suspected. When
he wanted money he had only to cut off a button.

The river Mawddach ran through the Dolgellau Gold Belt,
and its lower reaches have long been famous for excellent
salmon; a Victorian sportsman referred to the 'far-famed
Mawddach, one of the best if not the very best sewin and
salmon rivers in North Wales; anyone sceptical as to this
statement has only to stand upon Llanelltyd Bridge when the
net is being drawn, as it is occasionally, in the fine pool below,
to judge for himself.'

Waste products from the various gold and copper mines
near the river could be very harmful to the salmon, and though
every precaution was taken, accidents did sometimes occur. A
miner I knew was astonished to find a large number of salmon,
in the river below one of the mines, floating in the water,
apparently asleep. Though they moved off sluggishly when he
prodded them with his walking stick, they were obviously
half-doped. On making enquiries he found out that too much
ammonia, which was used for some process in the mine, had
been allowed to escape into the river, and the fish had been
nearly overcome by the fumes. That time they recovered.

Cascading noisily over the grey granite boulders through a
narrow valley, the river Mawddach once supplied power to the
Gwynfynydd gold mine. Now it is a very lovely place, for
native oaks, with ash trees and sycamores, abound; the ground
is carpeted with moss and fine grass and gradually the scars
made by the old mine are being obliterated by the

55

rhododendrons and silver birches which are springing up everywhere. Though dreams of wealth from the mines faded, wealth of another kind is now harvested along the upper course of the Mawddach, for the Forestry Commission have planted thousands of conifers. For miles the river runs through part of the huge forest which covers more than 18,000 acres and is one of the largest in Wales. It is called Coed-y-Brenin, The King's Wood, to commemorate the Silver Jubilee of King George V in 1935.

Gradually Japanese larch, Norway spruce and Sitka spruce, among others, are changing the face of the countryside and giving employment to numbers of local men who otherwise might have had to leave the district. Walking the many public footpaths in the Forest, every year a growing number of people are discovering the many attractions of Coed-y-Brenin, including the streams where trout lurk. Access has now been made easier to Pistyll Cain, the waterfall where the river Cain joins the Mawddach; Thomas Penant, who toured Wales at the end of the eighteenth century, wrote 'It is a cascade which astonished me with its grandeur. It formed a vast fall, bounded on one side by broken ledges or rocks, and on the other a lofty precipice.' It is indeed an awe-inspiring sight when in full spate the river Cain in a tremendous waterspout — which is what *Pistyll* means — crashes down from the rocky height to join the Mawddach far below.

Just off the main Dolgellau to Trawsfynydd road, past the little village of Ganllwyd, is Maescwm, a centre where the Forestry Commission explain some of the crafts of forestry to visitors, and have provided an artificially constructed little waterfall, where some of the many interesting plants which flourish in parts of Coed-y-Brenin have been planted. Prominently displayed is the following notice:

> Leave nothing but footprints,
> Take nothing but pictures,
> Kill nothing but time.

4

Customs Through the Seasons

Wales is a land of myths and legends, strange beliefs and superstitions which have come down to us on the tide of time from a past incredibly remote. Superstitions surrounded every aspect of life, some of the most interesting gathering round what have been called 'the rites of passage', the rites and customs woven round the three great events of human existence, where there is a passing from one stage of life to another, as marked at christening, marriage and death.

At a christening everything possible was done to ensure good luck for a baby. The north door of the church was left open so the devil could go out and the christening water was thrown out over the garden, on to something green, preferably the leek bed. But there was always the superstitious dread of a beautiful healthy baby being taken from its cradle by the *tylwyth teg*, the fairies, and a *plentyn-newydd*, a changeling, being left in its place. At first the *plentyn-newydd* looked the same as the stolen baby but gradually its appearance changed; it would become ugly, sickly and forever crying. To guard against this age-old terror, branches of the rowan tree or a piece of iron were placed near the cradle. Fairies were supposed to be frightened of red, so until well within living memory cradles were often hung with scarlet ribbons and pieces of cloth.

The very real fear of changelings has not yet entirely been forgotten. As a child in Merioneth, I was told the frightening story of a human baby stolen many years ago from a cottage near my home and of the dreadful little *plentyn-newydd* left in its place by the fairies. After many difficulties the mother found where her baby had been hidden, and managed to rescue it. I have often trudged up the steep path winding through the dark trees along which she is supposed to have dashed, her baby in her arms, the fairies in hot pursuit. There may have been solid foundations for the superstitions about changelings, for some folklorists think it possible that the *tylwyth teg* were originally a defeated people, driven by their conquerors to live in forests and uninhabited places, and if at any time their numbers began to dwindle, it may well be they stole strong, healthy babies from their conquerors, leaving sickly babies of their own instead.

In rural Wales, the community spirit has always been extremely strong, and the three great events of life were the concern, not merely of the immediate family circle but of the whole neighbourhood. Everyone gathered together, whether to mourn or to rejoice and there would be eating and drinking, and of course music.

As soon as the date of a wedding had been fixed, a bidder, or *gwahoddwr* as he was called, was sent from door to door, to invite the guests. He wore a white apron, with a wreath of flowers round his hat, white ribbons in his buttonhole and in his hand a long pole, or 'bidder's staff, with which he banged on the doors, claiming admittance. The *gwahoddwr* would have to walk many miles, so he carried a bag slung over his shoulder in which to put the food he was sure to be given.

Once inside a house he declaimed a long poem called a *rammas* or a *storiwawdd* — a bidding story — inviting everyone to the wedding and also pointing out that gifts would be most welcome — this was a very important part of the 'bidding'. The poem varied from place to place and from county to county; here is a prose version of part of an invitation given by a bidder at Llanbadarn in Cardiganshire:

With kindness and amity, with decency and liberality for Enion Owain and Llio Elys, he invites you to come with your goodwill on the plate; bring current money; a shilling, two or three, four or five, with cheese and butter. We invite the husband, and wife, and children, and men-servants, from the greatest to the least. Come there early; you shall have victuals freely, and drink cheap, stools to sit on, fish if we can catch them; if not hold us excusable. They will attend on you when you call on them in return.

After the introduction of the penny post, the bidding letter largely replaced the *gwahoddwr*, and though this custom had nearly died out by the turn of the century, in some remote parts of Wales it continued till World War I.

The night before the wedding was called 'sending Gloves Night', when friends brought their presents and also helped prepare the feast. On the wedding morning it was the custom in South-west Wales for the bridegroom and a party of his friends to call at the bride's house. The leader of the party, the seeker, or *gwyr*, knocked on the front door, whereupon a male relative put his head out of an upstairs window and asked what was wanted. The *gwyr* then demanded the bride and a verbal battle of wits, often in poetry, followed. Sometimes the bridegroom repeated these lines:

> Open windows, open doors
> And with flowers strew the floors:
> Heap the hearth with blazing wood,
> Load the spit with festal food,
> The chrochon on its hook be placed.

Eventually the *gwyr* got into the house and a wild search for the bride followed. When at last he found her, they ran off together, mounted on his horse and galloped off to the church, the bridegroom and the guests careering after them as fast as they could go, just like a pack of hounds after a hunted fox.

On other occasions the party set off quite decorously from the house on horseback — this was called *priodas geffylau*, a horse procession. Then without any warning, the bride's guardian, behind whom she was riding, instead of proceeding to the church would suddenly gallop off in quite another direction, pursued by all the guests. A mad chase across country ensued, fording streams, jumping hedges and ditches, chasing in and out of the narrow twisting lanes, and we are told that the women rode as wildly and enjoyed the impromptu steeplechase just as much as the men did. This went on until the bridegroom caught the bride. Although bad accidents sometimes happened — once the bride was drowned while crossing a river — these customs were still popular in the 1860s. The last recorded occasion was near Abergwili, Carmarthenshire, in 1876.

Many hazards seem to have faced brides in old Wales, and as a child I was told the story of a lady who lived at a farm so isolated that even today it is approached only by cart tracks. She had a fierce quarrel with the local squire, whose land surrounded hers, and she swore an oath that never again would she set foot on soil which belonged to him. But when she wanted to get married she was faced with an apparently insoluble problem — how was she to avoid breaking her oath and yet get to the church? The difficulty was overcome in a most ingenious way. A roll of white flannel was laid from her farm up to the road — she did not mind walking once there, for that was the King's Highway.

In some parts of Wales the putting of the ring on the bride's finger was the signal for all the young men to rush out of the church and run as fast as they could to the house where the reception was to be held, the prize being the wedding cake. This went on in North Wales as late as 1890. Even when the couple were married their troubles were not quite over, for often the churchyard gate was fastened against them — this happened at my parents' wedding at Caerphilly in 1903 — and not until handfuls of money had been thrown to the expectant crowd, would they be able to get away.

While the wedding meal was in progress a plate was handed round and each guest gave a present of money, a *pwyth*. Sometimes as much as £30 or £40 was collected, a handsome sum in the mid-nineteenth century. It used to be the custom at one time, shortly before the wedding, for the bride and her bridesmaid to call from house to house inviting their friends to the wedding, and then they collected presents at the same time. This old custom which was kept up in Cardiganshire as late as 1875 and was named 'calling in the *pwyth*'.

With today's easy motor transport, few people realise the immense trouble that had to be taken, well within living memory, in the remote mountain parishes of North Wales to arrange a funeral. Many farms were in such inaccessible places that no wheeled cart could reach them, so either the coffin was carried down by bearers — so their hands should not get chafed there would be specially wide handles — or on an *elor feirch*, a two-horse bier. This was rather like the stretchers now used by mountain-rescue teams, except that the handles were much longer, about 17ft, so there was plenty of room for a horse to be harnessed at either end of the bier, with the coffin securely lashed in the centre. The only two *elor feirch* known to survive are both in isolated Merioneth churches. The valley where Bala Lake stretches for four miles was often flooded in winter, making the few roads impassable, so coffins were taken by boat across the lake for burial in Llanycil churchyard, against which the waters lap ceaselessly.

As time went on people wanted a more convenient method for transporting the dead, and in Llanfachreth, my father's wild, sparsely populated parish among the grim mountains of north Merioneth, great annoyance was voiced at a vestry meeting in 1891 that there was no horse-drawn hearse, 'for lack of which the whole parish was suffering great trouble and expense'. So a Hearse Committee was formed, a Dolgellau carpenter agreed to make a hearse for £16, and a set of harness, 'really strong and hard wearing', was bought for £5. The parish was divided into six districts and collectors, laboriously covering great distances on foot, made house-to-house calls. Enough money was collected, and the hearse was driven from Dolgellau to Llanfachreth in triumph. It served the community till 1945.

An elaborate set of rules was drawn up for its use. It was free for any burial in the parish, whether church or chapel, the only charge being 1s 6d for cleaning it before a funeral. No special horse was used to draw it, anyone who had a strong, quiet one would lend it free of charge, but if, as sometimes happened, a dying person specially asked for a certain horse, that one was of course obtained. The Llanfachreth hearse was a very simple one, just a long, narrow, four-wheeled cart, painted black, in which the coffin was placed; nothing like the elaborate affair which belonged to Dolgellau in the 1890s.

Not everyone liked the new-fangled hearse, for soon after it had been bought, a fourteen-year-old girl, when she knew she was dying, implored her family to carry her. Her wish was granted and her coffin was carried the whole way to Llanfachreth church, a distance of about three and a half miles. The bearers, then as now, would have been the deceased's nearest male relations, the exact precedence based on degrees of kinship being worked out with great accuracy. When a young person was buried, the coffin was draped with a white cloth.

The hearse was no use in winter to farms high up in the mountains, which could be snowbound for weeks on end. At one such farm, during a terrible winter, an old man lay dangerously ill. Many feet of snow cut the family off from the outside world and the weather showed no signs of improving. *'Tad bach,'* (Father dear) the son said anxiously to the sick man, 'you can't possibly die now, for we shan't be able to get you away for weeks.' The sick man obligingly recovered.

At one time in Llanfachreth the 'last offices' were performed by a farmer. He never made any charge — it was just his way of serving the community. He was much surprised to have a letter from a solicitor in England concerning a man he had recently laid out. The old Welshman found the letter very difficult to understand for he 'had very little English', but at length he made out that the solicitor was settling up the dead man's affairs and wanted to know what were his fees. At first the farmer was reluctant to charge anything, but his friends eventually persuaded him to do so. How to describe, in English, what he had done? In Merioneth 'laying out' is called the *diweddu*, meaning an end or finishing, so after much thought an account was sent in 'for wash, brush up and finishing off'. The kind old man probably came across some curious things at times, for some women would have their wedding dresses laid beside them in their coffins, and some had quite valuable jewellery, or money, buried with them.

Before a coffin left a house, various ceremonies were customary. As soon as the news of a death became known, neighbours called on the bereaved, often walking many miles whatever the weather, carrying small gifts: a few eggs, a packet of sugar or some tea. Up to roughly the end of the last century, the night before the funeral, a *gwylnos*, literally a vigil or watch night, was held in the deceased's house. Friends sat up with the corpse through the night and there was a service with a sermon. This custom had ended by the turn of the century, and instead a short service was held in the house just before the coffin left, and if a mother had died in childbirth, leaving a baby, a 'coffin christening' took pace. A bowl of water was put on the coffin and the baby was literally christened over its mother's corpse — lest, I have been told, when the mother had gone no one would bother to baptise the baby. The last of these pathetic services that I know of took place in 1934.

A seventeenth-century writer records that in some parts of Wales, just before the funeral procession started, the coffin was brought out of the house and laid on a bier, beside which a man was standing. A loaf of bread and some beer was handed over the coffin to him, which he ate and drank, and he was given 6d. Then he hurried away by himself and hid from the sight of everyone, for he was the Sin Eater, who by partaking of food and drink over the coffin had taken unto himself 'all the sins of the defunct and freed him or her from walking after they were dead'. There is evidence that this macabre superstition lingered on in Carmarthenshire until the early part of the last century, in a slightly different form. There the Sin Eater entered alone into the death chamber, and after uttering incantation ate the bread and salt which had been placed on the dead person's breast. He was given a fee of 2s 6d and then hurried away, 'utterly detested in the neighbourhood — regarded as a Pariah — as one irredeemably lost'. Another form of the scapegoat of Biblical days?

When the mourners reached the church they divided, the women sitting on the right-hand side of the aisle, the men on the left, a custom only just discontinued. When the service was over, each member of the congregation put a silver coin in the offertory plate, placed in readiness on a black-draped stool in front of the altar. This silver collection, the *offrwm*, was always given to the priest, though my father used to return it to the relatives of the deceased. The Welsh word for a priest is *offeiraid* or one who offers; *offrwm* means literally an offering or a sacrifice, and one wonders if this custom dated back to pre-reformation times when money was offered to the priest to pray for the soul of the departed, or if it was rooted in some far older pagan form of worship, all traces of which have long ago been lost? The grave digger was given a copper collection, *arian Rhaw* — literally spade money, and he stood at the door of the church, holding his spade, to receive it. The popularity of the deceased was to a great extent measured by the amount of the collection and I well remember one sexton telling me that at the funeral of a woman who had led a somewhat curious life he only got 6s, but at the burial of a man who was respected and liked his collection amounted to £2 12s.

The most moving part of a Welsh funeral came as the mourners were waiting for the coffin to be lowered into the grave; as it moved downwards, effortlessly, spontaneously, unaccompanied, harmonising perfectly, everyone would break into a Welsh hymn, which I know from experience is heartrending in its beauty. This ancient, uniquely Welsh custom still survives.

Great numbers attended funerals and as many of them would have come a very long way, care was taken to provide a substantial meal. I had an old relation who had been an excellent housewife and when she lay dying she told her family which of the hams hanging up in her kitchen was in the best condition to be eaten at her funeral.

Curious terms were used to describe funerals. If a large crowd turned up it was called a 'strong' funeral and it was important for there to be a large number, for as someone once said to me, 'If you don't attend other people's funerals, how can you expect anyone to come to yours?' I remember a very important old lady being buried; everything had been done in the greatest style and, as was customary, the grave had been beautifully lined with moss and flowers. But she had not been liked, and the mourners said afterwards it had been a very 'dry' funeral, that is no tears had been shed. The actual funeral was not quite the end of the ceremonies attendant on death, for on the Sunday after the burial, at the evening service, a special sermon was preached in honour of the deceased, and the relatives, dressed in deepest mourning, attended in force, sitting in the front pews. They would walk incredible distances from the remotest parts of the parish, literally 'o'er moor and fen, o'er crag and torrent' to be present. Nearly all the customs I have mentioned have now fallen into disuse, but in Merioneth even today the actual ceremony of burial is considered so important that when there is talk of the departed, it is not the day the person died that is mentioned, but the date on which the funeral took place.

A curious Welsh custom relating to the rites of passage was the commemoration of these events by inscribed pieces of china. Once common in Wales, they are now seldom seen outside museums, but I have seen two inscribed christening mugs in a Merioneth house. The main colour is a striking shade of rich pink, with the rim and white handle ornamented with gold. A whole set of these mugs was made to commemorate 'Morris Pugh, Bodyfudda, born May 12th, 1885', the inscription being in gold lettering on a white background. I possess a cup and saucer depicting people in Welsh costume bringing wedding presents to an elegantly attired couple. The gifts include such useful items as a kettle, a broom, a ewer and jug, milking pails, and a warming pan, while in the background a man on horseback carries a large wooden chair.

The people honoured by commemorative china came from all walks of life, and mostly this was a nineteenth-century custom. The marriage of a clergyman was considered such an important event that a number of jugs were inscribed 'Long Life and Happiness To The Rev. J. Jenkins, Rector, Caerphilly, 1870' and given to people in the parish. The very handsome jug is cream coloured, the ornamentation on the lip and handle, the inscription and the very graceful bouquets of flowers on either side, all in gold. Some Merioneth friends of mine have a fine china hot-water jug with a metal lid. The jug is white with a band of bright pink; the inscription in gold states that 'Robert Parry Died July 2nd, 1878, Age 24. Not lost but gone before.'

The biggest and most elaborate funeral ever to take place in Wales, and probably in the United Kingdom, was when John Crichton-Stuart, fifth Earl of Dumfries, second Marquess of Bute, KT, and one of the largest landowners in South Wales, died suddenly at Cardiff Castle in March 1848; it is no overstatement to say that Cardiff was shattered, for Lord Bute had been the greatest benefactor the district had known.

(*above*) The Glasdir gold and copper mine, about 1910
(*left*) A cream-coloured jug commemorating the marriage of a rector, the Rev J Jenkins, 1870

(*above*) *Priodas yn Nghymru*, a wedding in Wales. Engraving dated 1853.
(*below*) The 'bidding' to a wedding, *Neithior yn Nghymru*. From an engraving dated 1853.

By the turn of the eighteenth century, the almost limitless mineral wealth in the nearby valleys of north Glamorgan had begun to be tapped, but no great quantity of coal could be exported, because the only outlet was the Glamorgan Canal, opened in 1794, and its sea-lock. Lord Bute, at some personal inconvenience, entirely financed the building of the first dock, later known as the West Bute Dock. It took exactly three years to construct, gave employment to hundreds of men, and was so well built that it was said to be 'capable of resisting the wear and tear of centuries'. Opened in 1839 it did not close till 1964. As a direct result, from being a small town of no importance Cardiff was well on the way to becoming one of the greatest coal-exporting ports of the world by the time Lord Bute died.

The elaboration of his funeral was not only because he had been a most distinguished and beloved man, but because he had left instructions that he was to be buried at Kirtling, a small village some 18 miles from Cambridge, in the family vault with his first wife, Lady Maria North, daughter of the third Earl of Guilford. The railway from London had not yet reached Cardiff, so it was decided to take the coffin by sea to Bristol, and thence by train to London. A night would be spent in the capital, then the corpse would be taken by train to Chesterford, 'where a grand procession will be formed and the whole will go to the place of interment at Kirtling'. Mr Banting, of Messrs Banting and Sons, Royal Undertakers, London, said the funeral procession was the most remarkable he had ever conducted, and never in the whole course of his experience had he ever seen such 'a large concourse of well dressed and respectable people'. He had managed the funerals of George IV, William IV and the Duke of Sussex, but there were quite twice as many people present at Lord Bute's funeral.

At 9.30 am the gates of Cardiff Castle were thrown open, and the vast procession began to move out. First came four policemen, then the Cardiff Amateur Band, all in deep mourning, their instruments draped with crepe and the drums covered with black cloth. Various societies came next, such as the Ancient Druids, the Odd Fellows, the Ivorites and the Cardiff Benefit Society — they all wore black scarves and white gloves, and some had black and white rosettes. They marched four abreast and were followed by fifty men employed by the great ironmaster Francis Crawshay, 'all of whom were supplied with silk hat-bands and black silk gloves by him; and further, he defrayed the expenses of their journey.'

A contingent of tradesmen and townsmen came next, followed by gentry marching four abreast, while behind them were the Royal Glamorgan Band and the band of the Royal Glamorgan Militia, followed by the Marquess's tenants marching four abreast, and the servants of the household in deep mourning.

Then came two mutes, 'a lid of plumes', a mourning coach conveying the late Lord Bute's coronet on a velvet cushion carried by his secretary, and then the hearse itself, drawn by six horses, 'hearse and horses being profusely covered with funeral plumes and rich velvet covering having the arms and supporters of the deceased Marquess emblazoned on either side with coronets, and crests on the back part.' A mourning coach drawn by four horses contained various members of the family, and after that was the family carriage, closed and drawn by four horses decorated with plumes, and numerous other carriages belonging to the important people of the district. The procession was 1½ miles long, was flanked on each side by police, and took three-quarters of an hour to pass a given point.

In heavy rain, immense crowds packed the streets all the way from the castle to the docks, a distance of some miles, and it is said that numbers of people were precariously perched on the roof tops. The Taff Vale Railway put on special trains early in the morning, so that thousands of people were able to come from the many little towns up the valleys. All shops and offices, public and private, were closed; private houses had their shutters closed and blinds drawn — the whole town looked as though a national calamity had taken place. Even the trains running to Cardiff were stopped, so that 'When the mourning procession passed along the side of the Bute Docks, scarcely a sound was heard except the solemn music of the Dead March in Saul, a well-known piece most appropriate to this solemn occasion, which contributed very materially in heightening the feelings of awe and solemnity which seemed to pervade the minds of all present.'

At the Bute docks, the ships with their colours at half-mast, the coffin was put on board the specially chartered Star steamer packet, followed by the chief mourners, for the voyage to Bristol. Lord Bute is commemorated in Kirtling church by a marble plaque, erected by his widow, Sophia Hastings.

Less than eighty years ago, cremation was regarded with something like horror. Even its legality was doubtful, and it is entirely due to the activities of an extremely eccentric Welsh doctor that the whole question was brought to the notice of the public and cremation made legal. William Price was born near Caerphilly, Glamorganshire, in 1800. He qualified as a doctor in 1820 and practised in various South Wales towns, being a popular doctor, but with advanced and unconventional views that upset many people. He was a vegetarian, advocated free love, held the legal system in contempt and was so deeply involved in the Chartist march on Newport, Gwent, in 1839 that, dressed as a woman, he had to flee to France and remain there for some years. He had no use for orthodox religion but claimed to be an Archdruid and performed strange rites by the Pontypridd rocking stone. Even his style of dress attracted attention, for he generally wore green cloth trousers, a scarlet waistcoat, a green cloth jacket or shawl and sometimes a white tunic. He always wore a cap made of fox skin with the brush hanging down his back. Though he did not believe in

71

marriage, when he was 83 he took Gwenllian Llewelyn into his household 'as companion', and by her had two children — a daughter Penelope and a son whom he called *Iesu Crist,* Jesus Christ.

In 1884 the son died and Dr Price tried to cremate the body, rather unsuccessfully, one Sunday evening in a field which belonged to him on the top of a mountain near Llantrisant. He put the body of the child wrapped in napkins, on the top of a huge cask full of paraffin and then set it all alight. It must have been a gruesome sight, and the large crowd which had assembled were so horrified at what they saw that they attacked the doctor, who might have been badly injured if the police had not arrived in time to rescue him. The charred body was recovered from the flames, and though at the inquest a verdict of death from natural causes was recorded, Dr Price had to stand trial at the Cardiff Assizes in February 1884, before Mr Justice Stephen. Dr Price had already been involved in innumerable lawsuits and was well used to conducting his own defence. So ably did he argue the case for cremation that not only was he acquitted, but Mr Justice Stephen declared that, provided it could be effected without causing offence or nuisance to others, cremation was a legal procedure. The trial, and the whole subject of cremation, aroused the greatest interest all over the country.

The doctor died at Llantrisant, near Cardiff, in 1893, at the age of 93. Those who saw the corpse say that, despite his great age, there was not a wrinkle on the face and his complexion was like that of a man in the prime of life. He had left minute instructions about the place and manner of his own cremation, which was to be on the mountain top, near where, at a second attempt, he had successfully consigned the body of his child to the flames. From designs drawn up by a well-known surveyor, a local blacksmith constructed a coffin of sheet iron, and iron bands were placed around it to prevent the body bursting out and being exposed to view. Along each side of the coffin were a series of holes, about 1½in in diameter, so that the fire could get more easily to the body and the gases emitted from the corpse could escape. The authorities went to enormous trouble to avert complaints on the score of indecency and nuisance. At 7 o'clock in the morning, twelve friends carried the doctor's body from his house to the funeral pyre; beside it was a large pole from which hung a flag with a crescent on it. Two Church of England clergymen conducted the service in Welsh, using the usual form for the burial of the dead, except that the body was 'consigned to the fire' and not to the earth.

By 3.30 in the afternoon the body had been entirely consumed; the remains were placed on a bier and taken back to Dr Price's home. Later, in accordance with his instructions, the ashes were cast 'to the winds and scattered o'er the earth to help the green grass and flowers to grow'. From early morning, people had been pouring into Llantrisant on foot and by train from the surrounding districts of Cardiff, Merthyr, the Rhondda and Aberdare, and it was estimated that by nightfall some 20,000 sightseers had come flocking into the little town. Five to six thousand attended the actual cremation and after it was over many of them searched among the ashes for relics.

A local doctor said on leaving the conflagration, 'It was a triumph for the doctrine of cremation, and in all probability this weird event which has taken place at Llantrisant will tend to popularise cremation among the working classes. It will not be a great event like this; the crowds have been attracted here simply because this is the first public cremation.'

Every season throughout the year had its special customs, but the most interesting are those connected with Christmastide and the New Year. From earliest times in the northern hemisphere the Winter Solstice has been a season of rejoicing, for then gradually the long winter nights begin to shorten and the days to lengthen. Man, completely dependent upon nature, then felt compelled to celebrate the growing strength of the sun, source of life, herald of the rebirth of plant life. Many Christmastide customs have roots stretching right back through the centuries to age-old fertility rites, and as Wales was so isolated, a number of very curious customs, elsewhere obsolete, lingered on there until well within living memory.

The Christmas season, *Y Gwyliau*, often lasted three weeks. Little could be done on the land and as a symbol of the suspension of work, the plough was brought into the farmhouse and placed beneath the kitchen table; but to show it was not forgotten, the plough was sprinkled with beer before anyone began to celebrate. In Carmarthenshire, on Christmas Eve, the boys and young men used to rush madly around, waving blazing torches from midnight till dawn. An old clergyman told me that when he was a child, he and his friends used to make an enormous ball out of all kinds of inflammable materials, stuck together with tar. Then it was set alight and rolled down the village street, the boys' fun being greatly enhanced by the efforts of the policeman to stop them.

The origins of fire-raising customs at Christmastide belong to the remote past. Suetonius Paulinus saw such ceremonies when he came to Anglesey in Roman times, but probably they date right back to the Celtic fire festivals held at the Winter Solstice to encourage the lifegiving sun to return. As for Christians this season meant the birth of Christ, the Light of the World; in Wales a very popular service was held at 3 o'clock in the morning to symbolise this. Boys bearing torches escorted the priest to the church; the congregation came carrying candles, large ones with very thick wicks to withstand draughts. Always many carols were sung and the congregation stayed till dawn, for the service was called *plygain*, dawn or cock-crow, when returning light banished evil spirits. In a different form, Montgomeryshire still celebrates the *plygain*.

Perhaps the greatest event at Christmastide was the ceremony of the *Mari Lwyd*, the Grey Mare. A horse's skull was mounted on a 5ft pole, enveloped in a sheet. Black cloth ears were sown on the head, the skull was gaily decorated with coloured ribbons, and pieces of glass were placed in the eye sockets. A man stood under the sheet and caused the grotesque horse to make terrifying snapping sounds, either with a wooden clapper or by clicking the lower jaw of the skull into which a spring had been fitted. A number of men accompanied the *Mari Lwyd* — one called the 'leader' led the horse with a pair of reins and when the party reached a house they intended to enter, he banged on the door with his stick.

The *Mari Lwyd* party sang verses which those inside had to answer; a great battle of wits ensued, and when the householders could no longer continue, the party was allowed to enter and was rewarded with money and refreshments. An old lady has told me that as a child her Christmases were quite spoilt by the fearsome-looking 'horse', which with its great snapping jaws chased her all over the big house where she lived. No one knows for certain the origins of the *Mari Lwyd*. Possibly it was a pre-Christian rite turned by the Church into a ritual celebrating the Virgin Mary, but after the Reformation gradually becoming a secular affair. According to a legend, the *Mari Lwyd* represented the horse that was turned out of its stable at Bethlehem to make room for Christ, and ever since it has been searching for shelter. Chiefly a South Wales custom, it gradually died out, but it visited Cogan Pill, my great-uncle's house, in 1914. 'Wassailing', when people called at houses and drank from a wassail bowl, continued in Gower until 1916.

Another custom widespread throughout South Wales was the wren hunt and procession, which took place on various days during the Christmas season, very often on 26 December, St Stephen's Day, because it is said that, by waking up his gaoler, a wren prevented the saint's escape. A wren was caught and put in a stable lantern or in a 'wren house', a decorated wooden box which was carried by a group of men from house to house where they would be entertained. My mother remembered this happening in the 1880s when she was a child, and how upset she was about the wren. As the hunt took place at the Winter Solstice, it may originally have been one of the rites practised by our remote forefathers to banish the evil influences connected with darkness.

Many curious practices were connected with the New Year. Mistletoe, so sacred to the Druids, was considered to be effective against poisons, fire and witchcraft and in Wales to ensure good luck for the dairy. The first cow that dropped a calf after the first hour of the New Year was given a spray of mistletoe. At Christmastime my mother and her sisters used to stay with their grandparents in a rambling, sixteenth-century house near Cardiff. Very early on New Year's morning, before anyone else was astir, the four little girls visited all the bedrooms in turn, where they were given a few pence. They carried an apple into which had been stuck pieces of oats, and on the top was a sprig of greenery, probably rosemary. The apple, on three sticks, represented the earth, the oats the life which would burgeon from the soil when the Winter Solstice had passed, the green sprig possibly symbolising a tree.

On Christmas Day a rather similar ceremony took place at Dynefawr Castle, Carmarthenshire, until World War I. A member of the family told me that after Christmas lunch everyone assembled in the great hall. The poorest women of varying ages, carefully selected from the village, came in and were allowed to choose either a large round of beef, a huge roll of Welsh flannel, or some blankets. In return, each woman presented my informant's grandfather with a rosy apple, garlanded with holly berries, on three wooden skewers. The apples were *never* eaten but were stored in the housekeeper's room till Twelfth Night, then thrown away.

It was customary in Wales to collect *calennig*, or a gift, on New Year's Day. Any child who called was given a penny, and I well remember this happening at various relations' houses in

Glamorgan. My grandmother gave each child a bright, new penny — carefully obtained beforehand from the bank. My uncle and aunt, who lived at the top of a mountain, gave a bun as well. The front gates were chained, the chauffeur and gardener stood on guard. Such a mob of children came, many carrying babies so they could collect an extra bun and penny, that the gates were only opened a few inches and about forty youngsters let through at a time. The noise they made as they surged and whooped up the long drive had to be heard to be believed. The record number was about 300 and the practice continued until World War II.

5

Witchcraft and Water

Amid the peace of the still unspoiled byways of Wales, in the brooding solitude of the mountains, there are still people who believe in the potency of witchcraft. Well within living memory there were people who, like their forefathers before them, practised mysterious ancient arts. A middle-aged friend has told me that as a boy he was ordered by his mother always to be polite to a certain woman, though she was disagreeable — otherwise she might lay a spell on him. When refused some milk by a farmer living near her, she had cursed him, saying, 'You would starve me, your cows shall starve you'. And soon afterwards things began to go wrong for the farmer; within a year he became bankrupt and shot himself.

I have a friend who hunted regularly in Pembrokeshire during the 1930s. Her horse, a sensible, stolid cob, could never be made to pass a certain cottage without great difficulty. He came from another county and no one but my friend had ridden him in Pembrokeshire, so she knew he had never had a fright while passing that spot. But in it lived an old woman feared by her neighbours. My friend was assured she was a witch, and as an example of her strange powers was told how one day her landlord had visited her on his way to market and had given her notice to quit. She abused him violently and finally cursed him, saying he would die shortly. Coming back that evening the man's dogcart overturned and he was killed instantly. No one ever again tried to evict the old woman, or to molest her in any way.

Through the long centuries in Wales, from the days of

Merlin until almost the present day, there could be found in many little villages a *dyn hysbys*, a wise man or conjuror, who with charms could cure diseases, protect animals and humans from witchcraft, remove curses and look into the future. When unaccountable illness struck farm animals, the best course was to consult a *dyn hysbys*. Some years ago an old clergyman told me that his father, a most respected farmer in Cardiganshire, would ride 25 miles to Llangurig in Montgomeryshire to consult a *dyn hysbys* if things went wrong on the farm. He always went at night and was very secretive about his journeys. The *dyn hysbys* had a number of different charms, one of which I have before me. The writing is so minute and the ink so faded that some of it is indecipherable, but the first part reads:

In the name of the Father, Son and Holy Ghost Amen x x x x In the name of the Lord Jesus Christ my Redeemer and Saviour I will relieve John Jones and Thomas Jones their Horses and Colts and Cows and Calves and all their creatures from witchcraft and from all evil men or women or spirits and from all the assaults of Satan, Amen. x x x x And this in all trust in the love of Jesus Christ that he will relieve the above Bodys from evil and craft.

The bottom part of the paper is covered with strange symbols and hieroglyphics, an astonishing mixture of paganism and Christianity.

An old friend of mine was a nonconformist minister, a highly intelligent, religious man of the utmost probity, but he firmly believed in witchcraft. He was brought up on his grandparents' farm in a hidden valley among the North Welsh mountains, so isolated that even today it has remained virtually unchanged. He was told the following story by his Aunt Catherine, like the whole family a truthful, God-fearing chapelgoer who also lived on the farm and was an eye witness of what occurred there in 1861.

One day the farmer was riding home and as he approached a steep hill a lame woman he knew asked if she could also have a ride. Politely he refused, saying that the mare was in foal and could not carry two people. The woman was extremely angry and cursed him. Early next morning the mare was found dead, though she had been all right the preceding evening; then one by one the cattle sickened and died, no one knew why. The farmer grew desperate and consulted a friend who told him the farm was obviously bewitched and the only thing he could do was to go immediately to a *dyn hysbys* at Towyn, some 20 miles away.

The farmer did not even go home first but set off straight away on the long walk to Towyn. As he approached his destination he became increasingly nervous. Would the *dyn hysbys* be in, would he mind his coming unannounced? But he need not have worried, he was welcomed in with the words, 'I was expecting you, I saw you coming — it is bad with you, isn't it?' The *dyn hysbys* told him his farm was bewitched by the woman to whom he had refused a ride, wrote out a charm for him, and put it in a sealed envelope, saying 'Keep this, and as long as it is in your possession, no one can cause you harm.' He also told him never to try and revenge himself on the witch, nor must he even *think* ill of her.

At the farm meanwhile, the farmer's wife and daughter Catherine were in a barn looking after a cow which was obviously dying. Suddenly there was a terrible noise and such a strong wind rushed through the cowhouse that the heavy threshing table in the loft above fell down. The girl was terrified, but her mother merely said, 'That's the old devil going away,' and at that precise moment the dying cow got up and began eating. Later it was found out that when this happened the farmer was actually receiving the charm from the *dyn hysbys*. No more animals died mysteriously on the farm, and as a child my friend saw the sealed envelope, kept most carefully in a chest.

I know the whole area well; the exact place where the encounter with the witch occurred, the lonely farm high up on the mountain, the old barn where the devil was raised — they are still there, little changed since my friend was a child, some 90 years ago. But what has always impressed me most about this seemingly impossible story is that the old minister gave me the names of everyone concerned, including the witch's, but made me promise I would never reveal them, as witchcraft is said to run in families, some of her descendants still live in the district, and he did not want harm to come to me.

A *dyn hysbys* was sometimes called in instead of a doctor. If a child with whooping cough visited a *dyn hysbys* three times and each time ate a cake he had made, the disease would be cured. The following is a translation of a Welsh charm widely used for toothache:

As Jesus walked through the Gate of Jerusalem, He saw Peter weeping. Jesus said unto him, why weepest thou? I have got the toothache. Jesus touched his tooth, And Jesus said have faith and believe, Thy tooth shall ache no more . . . I return you humble and hearty thanks for the blessing which You have bestowed on me.

The piece of paper on which the charm was written was rubbed along the tooth and the pain was supposed to go.

Only a few years ago I was talking to an elderly farmer who told me that in his father's lifetime the farm had been overrun by snakes, and nothing could get rid of them. A *dyn hysbys* said the only thing to do was to get soil from France and bury it in the fields around the farm. This was done and I was assured that the snakes vanished. Be this as it may, it is rather curious that the proper name for the farm, the one on the Ordnance Map, is never used; it is always referred to as *Ffranc* — the Welsh word for France. Also, round the farm in the fields, patches of soil quite different from the rest can be found.

Nowadays, of course, *dyn hysbys* have practically been superseded by doctors and veterinary surgeons, but even so, right up to the present day, I know of men who by means which defy rational explanation have cured people of diseases that baffled the medical profession. A couple of years ago a friend of mine had ringworm very badly and the doctor could do very little for him. He became so worried that he was persuaded to consult an old man living in Merioneth who was known to be able to cure the disease. He gave my friend some ointment which he saw being mixed on the lid of an old tin. He was told to return in seven days and by that time he was so much better that the old man said, 'We have killed the germ, now the skin must be made to heal' — and he was given a different ointment which soon completed the cure. The old man has died but he passed on his secret to a relation, who only last summer cured a child of the same trouble. A few years ago, a farmer I know well had an unsightly growth on his hand which in spite of medical treatment was gradually spreading. He consulted two well-known 'wise men', brothers, who lived in Caernarvonshire, and before long he was completely cured. Another friend of mine who had a facial growth was treated equally successfully by the brothers, who have recently died.

There used to be a number of people in Wales who could sometimes cure the *clefyn-yr-edef-wlan*, the disease of the woollen thread, so-called because of the means used to effect a diagnosis. The method used to vary a great deal; sometimes the sufferer had to take a special drink, sometimes the name of the Trinity was invoked, but in every case a piece of woollen yarn was used. It was measured and tied round some part of the body — leg, ankle, neck or arm. Later the thread was measured again; if it had lengthened the patient would recover, but if it had shortened he would die. I was extremely interested to hear the other day an account of this charm being used effectively only about ten years ago. A woman told me that her son, owing to overwork and worry, had a nervous breakdown and doctors could do nothing for him. He was persuaded to visit a *dyn hysbys* living in Mid-Wales, who without being told anything described the young man's symptoms exactly. He produced a piece of woollen yarn and measured it three times from the tips of the man's fingers to his elbow. The patient was told regularly to drink beer which had either a red-hot piece of steel plunged in it or was mixed with saffron. After a certain length of time the piece of wool was to be measured. The young man did this and found it had lengthened; he wrote and told the Wise Man who replied that now he was cured, and indeed he made a complete recovery.

These Wise Men charged no specified fee but left the amount to the discretion, and incidentally to the gratitude, of the patient. Money is a very secondary consideration with them, but one charmer on being given 2s 6d for having cured a growth did say, 'So that is what your life is worth to you.'

Inexplicable by rational means was an ancient cure for shingles, which apparently did work. The Welsh word for an eagle is *eryr* and the name for shingles is *eryri*, for this disease is supposed to have been introduced into Wales by a malevolent eagle. According to an ancient superstition those who had eaten eagles' flesh could cure shingles, and this power was transmitted down to the ninth generation. The charmer spat on the rash, rubbed his finger over the afflicted part and having breathed nine times over it, repeated the following:

> Male eagle, female eagle,
> I send you over nine seas, over nine mountains,
> And over nine acres of unprofitable land,
> Where no dog shall bark, and no cow low,
> And no eagle shall higher rise.

Some sixty years ago I can well remember a very old man whose father is said to have had this power. He lived in a tiny cottage right up in the mountains and one of his descendants who died only recently could remember seeing people toiling up the rough track to visit him. He insisted that they should come early in the morning, having fasted all the previous night.

Two other beliefs which defy rational explanation were firmly held by many Welsh people within living memory. In remote parts of Wales where tourists seldom come and the Welsh way of life flows on unchanging, old beliefs linger, old superstitions die hard, and the inexplicable still happens. The people who live in these places are hard-headed and practical; they have to be, in order to wrest a living from the unfriendly soil — and no one can bargain more shrewdly than a Welsh hill farmer — but there is an entirely different side to them as well; they live as it were in two worlds. For them the seen and the unseen, the material and the spiritual, exist side by side; and every now and then, the veil which hangs between the two worlds becomes transparent instead of opaque, and for a brief instant the invisible is seen and the inaudible heard.

There are stories from many different parts of Wales of *cannywll gorff* or corpse candles, little flickering lights sometimes seen near a house where someone is going to die, or perhaps at a place where a fatal accident will soon occur. The English name was 'fetch candles', lights sent to beckon or guide the living indestructible soul from the dying, destructible body. I know of several instances of these lights being seen near my old home in Merioneth, and I have talked to people of unquestioned integrity who have either seen them themselves or heard of them from eyewitnesses.

The northern part of my father's parish was especially isolated; few people went about at night, and if they did in such a small community it was known who they were and why they were abroad. One night an old woman lay ill and the girl who was looking after her had to leave her for a time to do the milking. When she had finished darkness had fallen, and as she went back to the cottage she was surprised to see a light bobbing along in front of her up the lane; just before she caught up with it, it went out. The old woman said no one had been to see her and from enquiries the girl made later, she found that none of the very few people who lived in the valley had been near the cottage that day, let alone after dark with a lantern. The next day the old lady died.

A very strong belief in the *cannywll gorff* existed in Pembrokeshire, especially in the diocese of St David's, and many stories of their appearance were told by people of the highest repute. They were mostly seen along the road by which a corpse would soon be carried for burial. One legend says that the lights appeared in answer to the prayer of a holy woman called St Lanon, who asked God that people might thus be warned of their approaching death and so have time to prepare for it. Another story is that when Bishop Ferras was burned at the stake in Carmarthen, he declared that if the faith for which he died was true, every person in the diocese of St David's would have their way to death lighted by a candle. A Pembrokeshire woman wrote in 1878: 'An old woman in Laugharne said to me she continually saw these lights. It seems from all I can hear, that they are seen as much as ever.' The writer goes on: 'Among the Greeks their appearances seem to have been known; for in Volume I, "Athenian Orachles," there is an account of the fetch lights or dead men's candles.' The last time a *canwyll gorff* was said to have been seen in my father's parish was in 1921.

There are also many instances in Wales of the strange power to 'foresee' funerals. I had a friend when I was a child whose father had this frightening gift. Sometimes when walking home in the evening along a narrow lane with a friend, he would suddenly step to the side of the road, pulling his companion with him. He explained that a funeral procession was passing and said so many mourners were on foot, and so many were riding; but the friend could see or hear nothing. Within the next ten days a funeral procession would indeed pass that way, the number of foot followers and horsemen would be exactly as the man had literally 'foreseen'. He lived near a churchyard and sometimes he would say he had seen a little light dancing over a certain spot; and sure enough, quite soon a grave was dug there. The old man apparently handed down his uncanny powers: I have known four generations of the family and in each there has been someone who could see into the future.

Mystery lingers still in the mountains of Merioneth. I myself know places amid the utter solitude of their desolate grandeur over which broods a silence so complete that it is almost tangible, where no dog will accompany one and where one has the overwhelming sensation of not being alone — in fact of being 'encompassed by so great a crowd of witnesses'. Sometimes these unseen presences are benign, but sometimes they are hostile as though they resent their solitude being invaded. Then one hurries away, without ever a backward glance.

Wales is a land of many waters; broad flowing rivers, turbulent mountain torrents, great waterfalls breathtaking in their beauty, mysterious lakes hidden away in secret places, magic wells. Often the mountain tops are shrouded in mist, sometimes the rain will fall for days and nights on end and the whole air is filled with the sound of water; water from the sky, water welling up from the sodden earth and water cascading down the mountainsides in twisted, silvery ribbons. Small wonder that in such a land strange beings were thought to dwell in the mists and by the rivers and that there are so many legends and beliefs concerning water.

Many waterfalls were thought to be haunted by the spirits of the unquiet dead or by the dreaded *Ceffyl-y-Dwfr* — the Water Horse. He looked like an ordinary horse and would allow himself to be mounted, but after a few moments he plunged into the depths of his watery kingdom where he devoured the unfortunate rider. Only a clergyman could safely ride a *Ceffyl-y-Dwfr*. In some parts of Wales the Spirit of the Mist was thought of as an old, grey-bearded man, *Y Brenin Llwyd*, the Grey King, who resided on the mountain tops where they merged into the mists. He seems to have been quite harmless, very different from the dreaded *Gwrach-y-Rhibyn*, the old hag of the mists and dripping fog, a greatly feared spirit which people have believed in almost within living memory. The swampy ground near Caerphilly Castle through which the *Nant-y-gledyr* runs was troubled by the hag, and as late as the 1920s an old man who lived in the neighbourhood remembered his father saying that he used to dread wet weather for then the marshy ground was transformed into a lake out of which the *Gwrach-y-rhibyn* with bat-like wings and long, black hair would emerge, and with weird cries vanish behind the castle walls. The old man swore that his father and other people had seen the apparition — 'true as the Bible it is'—and he also said that it never bothered newcomers to Caerphilly, only what he called 'the old stock'.

Stories about lakes are so widespread throughout Wales and follow such a distinct pattern that they may originate in pre-history, belonging to the earliest race memories of man. It has been suggested that the many tales of towns at the bottom of lakes refer to the prehistoric settlements of the Lake Dwellers. The recurring stories of mortals lured by fairies into the depths of those lonely, lovely, sinister stretches of quiet waters, hidden among dark mountain fastnesses, and the legends of marriages between land dwellers and fairy women emerging from lakes, might also be a race memory. As the stories concerning fairies and changelings, they could have been carried over from the time when the indigenous inhabitants of the land had been conquered by an alien people and were gradually absorbed by marriage and other peaceful ways, rather than exterminated. As nearly all stories of the *Twlwyth Teg* mention a horror of metal, it seems probable that the conquering race were the Iron Age people.

The story of Nelferch and Gwyn is a typical story of marriage between a fairy and a mortal. Among the mountains of Carmarthenshire lies Llyn-y-fan, in which, according to legend, lived Nelferch, a beautiful fairy. She was courted very ardently by a young farmer called Gwyn, and finally she consented to marry him, but said that she would return to the lake forever if he struck her three times with iron. He of course protested that such a thing could never happen. Nelferch brought with her a magnificent dowry of sheep, cattle, goats and horses. The marriage was ideally happy for many years, but accidentally Gwyn did strike his wife, and true to her word after the third time she called all the farm animals to her, and every one of them followed her to the lake from which they had emerged many years before, and disappeared into its black waters.

Gwyn was so broken-hearted that he drowned himself in the lake, and the three sons, distraught with grief, wandered round the lake, seeking their mother. One day she came to them and told them that their mission in life henceforth was to relieve suffering and cure all manner of diseases. She took them to a place which is still called Pant-y-Meddygon — the Hollow of the Physicians — where she taught them the healing properties of the various plants that grew there. She returned to the lake but reappeared from time to time and gave her sons such wonderful instructions and prescriptions that their fame as the Physicians of Myddfai was established throughout Wales.

As so often happens, this fantasy contains a germ of truth. Ample evidence exists that in Carmarthenshire during the thirteenth century there really was a family of highly skilled physicians, and that Rhys Grug, the Lord of Llandovery and Dynefor castle, gave them rank, land and privileges at Myddfai so they could practise their healing arts. Many of their ancient remedies have been preserved in writing and form an astonishing collection of strange cures and rules for a healthy life. Family tombs of the eighteenth century can be seen in Myddfai Church and descendants of the Physicians of Myddfai were certainly practising as doctors up to the outbreak of World War II.

In the very heart of Merioneth is a mysterious region

particularly haunted by legends and strange tales of long ago, and a lake which has two names and two personalities. Bala Lake is well known to hundreds of holidaymakers, and on a bright summer day, with children paddling, families picnicking round the edges, little boats bright with blue, white and red sails gliding over calm waters, glittering under an August sun, it looks ordinary enough. But on a dark winter day when the barren mountains which crouch round it like prehistoric monsters are crowned with snow and the grey waters are whipped to a fury by the winds blowing from the wintry heights, the lake assumes its other personality and becomes Llyn Tegid. Then one thinks of Tegid, a wise and mighty ruler who did much for his people, but who at the last was taken by treachery and drowned by his enemies in the lake, thus giving it its Welsh name.

One thinks too of the town which lies under the watery wastes, for according to legend Bala was a place of such iniquity that at length the patience of heaven was exhausted and it was overwhelmed by a great flood which drowned everyone except a good old harpist, who warned by a bird fled to the safety of the mountains. When day broke, where once had been a prosperous city all that could be seen was a great lake and floating on it was the old man's harp. The exceptionally heavy rainfall in this region might be blamed for the number of watery legends; according to an old Welsh story, the Flood itself was caused by a monster bursting out of Llyn Tegid and it was near here, and not on Mount Ararat, that Noah's Ark came to rest. A year or so ago I heard of an old lady — she had only died a few years before — who as a child had been taken by her grandmother to see a certain large stone not very far from the lake, on it were said to be all kinds of different marks made by the feet of the various animals as they emerged from the Ark.

According to some legends Cahir ap Cynyr, the Sir Kay of Arthurian romances, lived near Bala Lake, and King Arthur himself was brought up in the vicinity by his foster-father. Yet another legend says his early years were passed near Llanuwchllyn, the little village to the west of Llyn Tegid; nearby is a cave where, surrounded by his knights, he sleeps until the appointed hour of awakening. Tennyson is thought to have stayed at Bala when composing part of *The Idylls of the King*; indeed he says that love grew in the King's heart:

> As the south west that blowing Bala Lake
> Fills all the sacred Dee.

West of Bala Lake amid the desolation of Ddallt, the mountain that forms a watershed between east and west Merioneth, lies the source of the river Dee which from the dawn of history was worshipped as a sacred stream. Even when with the coming of Christianity numerous little churches, two important monasteries and a cathedral were built near its banks, it was still regarded with superstitious awe. Its very name is probably derived from the Welsh word *Duw*, meaning God, and many poets have referred to the sanctity of the Dee. Spenser in his poem about the rivers attending the marriage of the Thames and the Medway wrote:

> and following Dee, which Britons long ygone
> Did call Divine, which both by Chester tend.

Drayton often uses the phrase 'Dee's holiness', and Milton in his *Lycidas* says 'Where Deva spreads her magic stream.' Once, before engaging in a vitally important battle, the Welsh bowed their knees to the ground and each drank from the sacred waters of the Dee. The river is said to flow through Bala Lake without merging with its waters.

Some three miles north of Dolgellau lies another enchanted lake. Llyn Cynwch, in its utter solitude surrounded by mountains, seems an idyllic place, but many years ago legend says, a huge serpent lived nearby. It terrified the whole neighbourhood, for any living creature that looked into its eyes was paralysed and then devoured. It became such a menace that the Lord of Nannau, in whose land the lake lay, offered a reward of sixty cattle to anyone who could slay it. One day Meredith, a shepherd, accompanied by two dogs, was passing Llyn Cynwch when he came upon the serpent, fast asleep. Leaving the dogs to keep guard, he hurried off to Cymer Abbey a few miles distant, borrowed an axe from the monks, returned to Llyn Cynwch and with the help of the dogs killed the serpent. He buried the carcase somewhere on the lonely heights of a mountain overlooking the lake. On the Ordnance Survey map it is marked 'Foel Cynwch', but it is still the custom for local people to use its older name, *Carnedd-bedd-y-wiber*, the Grave of the Serpent.

There is another grim story about the lake. It is supposed to be the haunt of a being in the semblance of a man who emerges from the water crying, 'The hour has come but not the man,' and if any unfortunate person is passing he is dragged into the depths, never to be seen again.

Not surprisingly, fairies haunted this lovely stretch of water. One evening Owain, a servant from a nearby house, went to visit his sweetheart who lived some miles away. Passing Llyn Cynwch, the night was so dark he missed his way and fell into the lake. Down and down he sank, but to his surprise he could still breathe quite well, and when he eventually reached the bottom he found himself in lovely country. A little man appeared and guided him to a magnificent palace, its towers soaring up to an azure sky, more wonderful than anything Owain had ever envisaged even in his most exalted dreams. The palace was full of lords and ladies who made him welcome and entertained him to a sumptuous repast. Then Owain remembered his sweetheart and said he must hurry away or she would wonder what had become of him. So the same little man who had been his guide said he would show him the way home.

He led Owain through a long tunnel until they came to a flight of stairs. The young man bade his guide a grateful farewell, climbed the steps, opened a trap door at the top, and to his amazement found himself standing on the hearthstone of his sweetheart's home. She greeted him as one who had returned from the dead, for he found that, instead of having been away for only a few hours as he supposed, it was many months since he had left, and he had been given up for dead.

Many legends have accrued around the many wells that can be found throughout the length and breadth of Wales. Some of the wells were important in pagan times, and with the coming of Christianity were taken over by the Celtic church and turned into healing or holy wells. Many were said to be of miraculous origin, having sprung up in answer to the prayers of a Celtic saint, like the one near my home in Merioneth. St Machreth, the patron saint of Llanfachreth Parish, had a small dwelling in a wood. Many holy men came and stayed with him, among whom was St Gwynog, who to show his gratitude for the hospitality he had received caused a spring to issue from the ground. The legend goes on to say that he blessed the spring, and from then on the water possessed miraculous powers, healing all kinds of complaints, especially anything to do with the eyes. Within living memory the moss that grows near the well, and is impregnated with its water, was used to bathe the inflamed eyes of people and horses. The well can still be seen. At one time a sect of Baptists used to come from many miles away to be baptised in the water, which like most reputedly holy water flows southwards. According to The Royal Commission on Ancient Monuments, County of Merioneth, Volume VI, September 1913, 'The well enclosure is 19 feet 6 inches square, and has a flight of five steps to the water level. It is now chocked with vegetable growth, but the spring must have been credited with medicinal virtues, otherwise so ample a bath would not have been provided.'

As late as the 1920s water from the spring was still being used for all christenings in the church.

The prosperous town of Holywell in North Wales owes it origins to a fantastic legend. Winifred, a saintly and beautiful maiden, was annoyed by the amorous attentions of a Prince Caradoc. One day when out walking he tried to rape her and was so infuriated when she managed to repulse him that he struck off her head which went rolling down a hill. Where it came to rest a spring of clear water sprang up, forming a deep well. By a lucky chance, Winifred's uncle, St Beuno, happened to be there. He promptly stuck his niece's head on, doing it so neatly that only a thin red line showed where she had been decapitated, and she lived another fifteen years. A great chasm appeared and swallowed Prince Caradoc up.

A tremendous cult developed around St Winifred and her well, which was supposed to have miraculous curative powers. A religious community sprang up near it which became immensely wealthy from the thank-offerings given by the pilgrims who came in thousands. Among distinguished visitors were William the Conqueror, Edward I and James II, who in August 1686 paid his respects to the saint and was given the actual shift in which his great-grandmother, Mary Stuart, had been executed. Even as late as 1850 a visitor records, 'In the summer numbers bathe here, and many hand-barrows, crutches, chairs, etc. are hung up in the interior [of the shrine] as offerings and as proofs of the efficacy of the waters. There are ugly boxes for bathers inside, and a bath outside 4 feet deep — the water never freezes and does not vary, and the astonishing quantity of 84 hogshead is thrown up every minute.'

In some parts of Wales, even ordinary rain water was thought to have magical properties. Only the other day a friend told me she can remember her grandmother putting out a bowl to catch 'the first shower in May'. The water was carefully stored in a bottle and used for sore eyes.

6

Old-style Craftsmen and Farmers

Those who know where to look can still find hand craftsmen of rare skill, like Robert Griffiths, known to his many friends as 'Bob Bach'. He lives out of sight of the road in a secret glade overshadowed by magnificent beech trees in a caravan he designed himself. His job is with the Forestry Commission, but his leisure time is spent in his little workshop making all manner of things in wood with infinite skill and patience.

A visit to Bob is an unforgettable experience; it is also a journey back into the past, for as you toil up the narrow, lost valley to his home and workshop, where after dark he works by the light of an oil lamp, time seems to play a trick on you, the present slips away and there is a feeling of having stepped back into a bygone age, an age when mass-produced goods were unknown.

Everywhere there is evidence of Bob's skill. He makes hafts for axes; farmers come great distances to buy his rakes which are made entirely by hand, generally from ash wood. To the uninitiated it looks as though the top of the hay rake is made of three separate pieces of wood, but in reality only one piece is used. It is very carefully split down the middle for about ten inches. The top layer of the wood is split again, and these two parts are then bent outwards with great skill. Then all three pieces are eased into the head of the rake in which hand-made teeth or pegs have already been fitted. Bob makes rakes in different sizes, for men, women or children, the number of pegs ranging from 19 to 13. For just a few friends he will make tiny rakes, exact replicas of the full-sized ones.

Bob sometimes carves a magnificent chair for a local Eisteddfod; sometimes a gate for a farmer. But he often creates things not for sale, just for the sheer joy of the work. In his workshop one day I found it full of beautiful things. In one corner stood a carved oak standard lamp; on a shelf, half hidden by a pile of tools, was a cigarette box, its sides dovetailed together with exquisite precision; tucked away on another shelf among some spade handles was a beautifully made miniature Welsh dresser, in finest oak, with three sturdy shelves and drawers and cupboard doors that opened at a touch.

Some of the tools Bob uses, like the strange-shaped axe called locally a *neffau,* are very old. A *neffau* has a long, curved blade several inches wide, and to handle it requires special skill; few people are left who have it. The user stands with one leg each side of the piece of wood he is chopping, swinging the *neffau* between his legs.

Bob comes from a family of craftsmen and never had to leave home for his apprenticeship — he learned from his father and grandfather who were well-known over a wide area for their superb carpentry. Even today one comes across evidence of their skill in out-of-the-way places. I know a cottage where there is a magnificent oak dresser, well over two hundred years old, so skilfully mended by Bob's father that only the owner can point out the repairs. People were still churning by 'dog-power' when I was a child, and a friend of mine in 1916 can remember seeing two bitches churning butter by means of a wheel, rather like a huge turnspit, placed at an angle a few feet from the ground. The wheel — Bob's grandfather had made it — was started off by hand and then the dogs could carry on quite easily, taking about three-quarters of an hour to make the butter.

Bob has been offered various good jobs in England, but he will not leave his valley, for he prefers to live out his life doing the work he loves, just as the spirit moves him, among his lifelong friends, enfolded by the profound peace and unspoiled beauty of this remote valley where so many of his people have lived and died.

Another skilled craftsman is Glyn Rees, who for many years has lived in the little Merioneth village of Dinas Mawddwy, and like his father and several generations of forbears, has spent nearly all his life working in wood. In common with other fine craftsmen, he has no need to advertise, indeed he shuns publicity. His workshop is out of sight and difficult to find, but it is well worth a search for one is welcomed there with true Welsh kindness and hospitality.

Glyn is always pleased to show you round the large, airy place, where from oak and many other kinds of timber, including pitch pine and mahogany, he fashions a wide variety of beautiful and unusual things. He makes long-backed spinning chairs, bellows of every size — some quite small, others with handles several feet long — dressers, cupboards, coffins — he is also an undertaker — chests, and stools, some covered with leather, others with tapestry woven locally. A massive oak door, studded with nails, was going to an old house in Machynlleth, and I noticed a charming little drop-leaf table, the top of which could be securely locked by just giving it a half turn. He excels in fashioning church furniture, examples of his work can be found in a number of churches in North and Mid-Wales, particularly in the Bala area.

His wood must be properly seasoned. One way of clearing out all the sap, particularly in oak, is to drop the timber into a pond and to leave it there, possibly for as long as a year. In the old days, wherever there was a sawbench there was also a waterwheel, and where there was a waterwheel you found a mill-pond. Sawn planks were put into the pond and left there to float for three or four weeks. Glyn told me of the very valuable oak that is occasionally turned up by drainage excavations from deep down in boggy ground, where it may have lain for as long as 1,000 years. Black as ebony, though possibly not so hard, it makes wonderful furniture. Indeed, it is so valuable that a few unscrupulous antique dealers have been known to bury ordinary oak in the right kind of marshy ground, and then sell furniture made from it as the more expensive bog oak. Glyn is fortunate in that his son Dilwyn, who works with him, promises to be another fine craftsman.

Through the long centuries Wales has been famous for cattle and dairy products and among the commonplace sights of my childhood were cows being milked by hand in little stone barns, and butter being churned, also by hand, on the farms. These age-old crafts can seldom be seen now and an urban generation has grown up which has never drunk warm, fragrant milk straight from a cow, or tasted completely fresh, hand-churned butter. But there are just a few places where these delights can still be sampled. A couple of years ago, one August Bank Holiday, I was sitting on the lower slopes of a mountain gazing into the valley below. No holidaymakers, not a car to be seen or heard, just the valley filled with long shadows and the luminous light of the westering sun, while in the distance stark mountains were already beginning to darken. Except for a few sheep tearing at the fine turf the silence was absolute. Presently it was broken by the old cry of 'buwch, buwch', accompanied by shrill whistling calls, and round the edge of the mountain came John Lloyd, always known as Non Ty-isa, with his black-and-white sheepdog, to collect the cows from higher up the mountain for the evening milking in the valley below. The Welsh Blacks were an arresting, strangely primitive sight, when a few moments later, with a pounding of hooves, they came galloping down the mountainside. Silhouetted against the evening sky, with horned heads tossing, tails held high and streaming behind them like banners, they resembled a huge, animated frieze from a bygone era very far removed from our mechanised age.

A few days later I talked with Non as he did the milking in a stone barn that had withstood many a harsh Welsh winter. The weather had changed completely and a chill wind laden with rain was blowing from the east. Sitting comfortably enough on a truss of hay, taking in the nostalgic smell of cows and hay, the sounds of the rhythmic ping of the warm milk frothing into the metal can and the occasional rattle of a chain as a cow moved her head, I listened also to Non's soft Welsh voice telling me about his cows and his small farm where he had lived all his life and successfully brought up a large family. Though his cattle have passed the required tests he does not sell milk but keeps it for his family's requirements.

In a very few old farms like this, one still sees butter being made in the traditional way. The Lloyds' house was largely rebuilt in 1808, so it is comparatively modern as things count in rural Wales, but the semi-basement dairy with its 3ft thick walls, stone-flagged floor and slate shelves, is far older. There one afternoon I found Non's wife Menna churning the weekly supply of butter. The churn had only been bought some thirty years ago — a good one will last a lifetime — but the wooden bowl, and the spoon with the traditional design carved on it, had been in Menna's family for countless years. Old too were the huge earthenware crocks in which butter was stored for use during the long, cold winter months. Butter made in September kept the best; extra salt was mixed with it and it was put into crocks with a thick layer of salt laid on top. Our winter supply was stored in our larder — as cold as any refrigerator — and kept perfectly well into the spring.

For making butter, milk has to stand for about three days, the exact time depending on the weather. Most people had a separator, a machine for separating the cream from the milk, but Menna had no such mechanical aid; like her mother and grandmother before her, she used a saucer to skim off the cream from which the butter would be made. The milk that was left over is called 'buttermilk' and these days is fed to the calves, but years ago it was considered a very palatable drink.

The afternoon I watched the churning was sultry but at last a 'plopping' sound told that the butter was being formed. The churn was opened and a bucket of water thrown over the butter to wash off any surplus milk, and then drained away by a tap at the bottom of the churn. The butter was placed in a large wooden dish and turned, kneaded and pressed by hand for almost as long as the churning took, because if any moisture at all was left it would not keep but would turn rancid. Then salt was added and the butter had to be worked until all the minute air bubbles had disappeared and it was perfectly smooth. Next the butter was weighed into pounds and slapped into shape by rectangular pieces of wood with long handles, oddly enough called in Wales 'Scotch hands'.

We often hear someone say, 'What an unusual character so-and-so was, they don't come like that these days', but in places among the mountains and in lonely valleys men and women can be found who are just as unusual as any who went before them. Running a small farm and carrying the post for many miles in a lonely district are unusual occupations for a middle-aged woman, but it is a way of life my friend Mari Jones enjoyed. She and her sister have lived nearly all their lives in a small stone cottage called Doladd, hemmed in by trees which cannot even be lopped because they were planted by their long-dead mother. Doladd lies in a narrow valley; there is no habitation within sight, only mountains, woods owned by the Forestry Commission and a few fields.

There are no modern conveniences in the cottage, no mechanical aid on the farm. Only a little corn is grown and that is fed, unthreshed, to the few cows that keep the sisters well supplied with butter. Regardless of time, my friends will work far into the night if the weather is fine and there is work to be done. One summer evening some years ago, I was passing down their tranquil valley; to the west the mountains stood black against the sunset sky, and the first stars were beginning to tremble in the deepening dusk. The sisters were still busy with the hay — they had been at it when I went up the valley at midday and I knew they would carry on under the light of the August moon till the small hours of the morning. Hard work it was too; they had no horse, so they carried the hay in sacks on their backs to the huge, stone barn.

Their fifty sheep are no ordinary animals, for unlike Welsh sheep which by English standards are unbelievably wild, these are quite tame and come when called. This is fortunate, for one year when the flock had to be taken to the distant sheep walk, the dog was not well enough to shepherd them, so she stayed in comfort by the kitchen fire while, nothing daunted, the two ladies set forth on their own with the sheep. They managed perfectly well — one walked in front like a patriarch of old, and the other brought up the rear.

For sixteen years Mari also carried the post. Each weekday at 11 o'clock, the mail van called for her, took her three miles up the valley into the heart of the mountains, and dropped her at an old stone bridge. She began her round along a road where once the Roman legions tramped, but soon struck off along a footpath. She carried the mail by streams where otters still whistle at night, across desolate valleys where buzzards wheel and mew and through dense Forestry Commission plantations. 'Mari the Post' used to reach home about 4 o'clock in the afternoon. She took no food with her, nor would she accept any while on the rounds, but would sometimes have a cup of tea. During the sixteen years she said the worst time she experienced was during the terrible winter of 1947. At one farm she visited a tunnel had been dug through the snow from the house to the cowshed, and even

(*above*) The coffin of the Marquess of Bute was loaded on to a specially chartered steam packet at the Bute docks, Cardiff, to be taken to Bristol en route to London.
(*below*) Bala Lake, from a mid-19th-century engraving

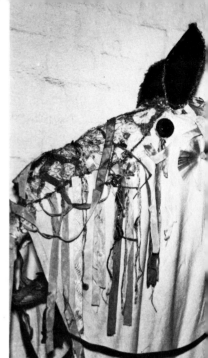

(*above left*) Some of Glyn Ree's handiwork
(*above right*) *The Mari Lwyd* (Grey Mary) used in Christmas revels
(*right*) 'Bob bach' in his workshop

on her own fields, down the valley, the snow lay deep for seven long weeks.

Three most unusual old men died only recently in the Parish of Llanfachreth. I knew Llewelyn Evans, or 'Llew' as everyone called him, since I was a child. He was one of ten children, all handsome, most of them talented musicians or poets. The only education Llew received was at the village school and nearly all his life was spent in the little cottage over 1,000ft up in the mountains. There were two distinct sides to Llew's character. He was a shrewd, successful farmer, running his farm without any machinery, with the help of only one man, and well-known as a breeder of fine rams. I saw him only a few days before he died, and the first thing he whispered to me was 'How are the rams?' One summer, after toiling up a precipitous, stony track, when I eventually reached his farm I felt as though I had stepped straight back into my childhood, for across the hay fields, illuminated by the evening light, came my old friend leading his mare. She was pulling one of the very old-fashioned wheelless wooden sledges which looked like an inverted bedstead, piled up with hay. They were in common use years ago, but are now practically obsolete.

That was Llew the farmer; but there was also Llew the musician, who trained the village choir for countless years; who won recognition and high awards for his unique collection of folk tunes which otherwise would have been lost to posterity. Two miles from Llew's home is a church, and Llew walked there and back, every Sunday morning and evening to play the organ for half a century, a span of years which must be a record even in a land of musicians. At many times there was extra pressure of work on the farm, or sickness at home, or the snow lay deep or torrential rain or blinding mists were sweeping over the mountains, and then the miles to the church must have seemed long but Llew never faltered. Always at church-time his tall figure could be seen striding manfully along the winding road, his bowler crammed firmly on his head, his raincoat flapping in the wind, a large umbrella in his hand. In Wales no one can be buried or married without music, so often on a weekday too, the old church was filled with the wonderful music of Llew, the self-taught musician. Even when he gave up his post as organist, among the mountains, in his little cottage which has stood foursquare to the snow and rain and bitter, howling winds for well over a hundred years, this gifted man went on studying and making music on his little organ till he died.

As there are few Welsh surnames, people are called after their job or by the name of their farm, like Hugh Williams, always known as 'Hughie Ffriddgoch'. Until he died a couple of years ago at the age of eighty-six, he was running his little mountain farm with the aid of a brother and sister only a little younger than himself. Like my other friends, he had no mechanical aids on the farm but lived much as his forefathers had done before him. The hay was cut with a scythe and then taken in a horse-drawn sledge and stored in an enormous stone barn. The farm is so isolated that even today only a cart track leads up to it; coal was dumped as near as possible and was then transported to the farm in a small sledge drawn by a horse which, if animal years could be estimated, was as old as her master. Hughie Friddgoch did not believe in 'newfangled' cattle nor mechanically operated 'milking parlours'; Welsh black cattle grazed in the quiet pastures and on summer evenings were milked in the open.

It was a hard life but Hughie Ffriddgoch found time to walk to chapel every Sunday morning and teach in the Sunday School in the afternoon. He had only attended school for a few years but went on educating himself all his long life, and though he had no piano he was well-known for the melodious hymn tunes he composed, harmonised with great skill into four parts, which were often used in his chapel — one was sung at his funeral. He was the fourth generation of his family to live in the small, late-eighteenth-century stone cottage, tucked against the hillside and slightly protected by an enormous Scotch fir from the fierce winds that funnel up the valley.

Another lifelong friend was John 'Siop', so called because for over forty years he ran the village post office and general shop, and even when he retired, the name still clung to him. He spent his childhood in a little stone cottage on the edge of a sombre fir wood, haunted by dark legends of witches and malevolent fairies. There was little money; John's father supplemented his tiny weekly wage as one of the woodsmen on the local squire's estate by keeping poultry, a pig and a couple of cows. When autumn came and it was too cold for the sheep to remain on their customary mountain sheep-walks, he would take in about twelve animals for other farmers at 1s 8d per head for the whole winter. Now the charge would run into pounds. Though the only formal education John ever received was at the village school, which he left when aged thirteen, there was little he could not turn his hand to, either on a farm or with anything to do with machinery. His first job was in a little gold mine, a stone's throw from John's home across a deep chasm through which a turbulent mountain stream swirled. For a number of years John travelled the district with his uncle's horse-drawn threshing machine, then he gave that up, married and settled down.

For many years he successfully ran a small farm and the village shop. When he took over in the early 1920s, there was no public transport to the nearest town, four miles away. Bread was the only commodity to be delivered, so the whole of the little community was dependent on him, and never once in all the long years was that trust betrayed. The shop kept open late in the evening, for nearly all the customers were busy on the farms during daylight, but it did close for a short time about five o'clock so that John could do the milking. It was a charming sight to see the cows walking behind their master down the village street from the field to the milking barn, for John had trained successive generations of his cattle to follow him like dogs.

If people fell on evil times and money was short they were never pressed for payment; when the Post Office telephone was the only one in the village, John was always ready to deliver a message whether urgent or merely frivolous. As a prominent member of the local chapel, John was always busy on Sundays.

Before World War I, the customary life of a priest in an isolated parish like my father's among the mountains of north Merioneth was a hard one. But he preferred it to any other way of life. Year after year, day and night, whatever the weather, he was on call, for in those days few adults cared to die without a priest, and it was unthinkable that a sickly, newborn baby should die unbaptised, for it was believed that otherwise its soul passed into limbo. Like other parsons in remote, sparsely populated districts, Father knew personally every man, woman and child committed to his care, and in a way which is impossible today was deeply involved in their lives and with the cycle of the seasons. He was looked up to and his advice was asked on a wide variety of subjects, secular as well as spiritual.

On Sundays he took four services, one in English, the rest in Welsh, and preached three sermons, but occasionally he also rang the bell himself or played the organ, for both the bell-ringer and the organist lived a long way away and could not always come. Father was extremely musical; sometimes his own hymn tunes were sung in church, but he had little time to devote to composing.

Most weekdays were spent in visiting, for Father thought that this was one of the most important duties of a priest. Though the population was small, it was so scattered, and some of the farms so isolated, that calling on just one family could mean a day's journey. As there were no cars nor public transport in those days, he rode everywhere on his stout Welsh cob, along rocky mountain tracks, through dark woods and over desolate moors, wearing his usual clerical garb and an Inverness cape if it was raining hard or snowing. When he could no longer afford to keep his horse, he walked instead.

Single-handed he kept the enormous vicarage garden in some kind of order, and in spite of the depredations of rabbits, pheasants, the neighbours' sheep and an occasional cow, and the very cold, wet climate, he grew all our vegetables. For many years, until the dreaded Isle of Wight disease decimated his hives, he was a most successful apiarist, in one year alone selling over 300lb of wonderful heather honey in Barmouth. Our water supply came from two tanks up the mountain behind the vicarage; quite often something went wrong with it and there was no water, and whatever the trouble was, it was Father who had to put it right for there was no plumber within a day's journey, ours being the only house with water laid on. Nor was there any professional chimney sweep; when really necessary Father cleaned the chimneys, by the simple expedient of setting them alight. In his spare time he did carpentry jobs, like making or mending his beehives, or with a large cross-cut saw and my assistance he cut up logs for the long, cold winter. If in the summer a farmer was short-handed with the hay and the weather looked threatening, Father would willingly help all day until the fields were cleared.

A good classical scholar he taught my brother and me until we went to boarding school. Besides formal lessons, as we walked round the parish with him he taught us about the numerous wild flowers and the animals we saw, explained the geological formations, and often on starlit winter evenings, well muffled against the bitter cold, would take me into the garden to pick out the major constellations, Orion, Ursa Major,

107

Cassiopeia, and learn the legends connected with them.

He had a keen sense of justice, and fear of unpopularity never deterred him from rebuking those in high places when he thought it necessary. A parishioner who had managed a farm lost the job, through no fault of his own, because the landlord wanted to put in a friend of his instead. The offer of another farm was useless to him for he had no money to buy stock. No one could help him, so in despair he came to Father, who though a poor man himself at once lent him sufficient money to buy a few cattle, and my mother advanced him enough to get a small flock of sheep. Over the years the money was gradually and meticulously paid back in kind: in meat, butter, eggs and so forth.

One spring during World War I, when the country's food supplies were desperately depleted, Father revived the custom of the ancient church of blessing the crops on the three days immediately before Ascension Day. The parish was so large that it was not possible to visit the boundaries, as had been the old custom, so three places at widely different points of the compass and not too far from the vicarage were chosen. Father in his cassock and surplice, followed by a small band of parishioners, walked to the appointed places where a few prayers were said, the crops blessed and a hymn sung. These services were much appreciated by the farmers.

My father has been dead for many years, but there are still many who remember him with affection and respect.

7

The Old County Town and the Wild Route to Bala

There are few big cities in Wales but many interesting little towns like Dolgellau, the county town of former Merioneth. Guarded by mountains, it is situated in so lovely a place that when George Fox, the Quaker, first saw it, he said he had found an earthly Paradise and that 'here is a valley of peace and beauty'; Bronze Age people lived on the mountain, the valley echoed to the tramp of Roman soldiers, Christian missionaries founded a settlement there in the seventh century and four hundred years later came the invading Normans under the command of William Rufus, who an old chronicle states 'returned empty handed having gained nothing'.

Little is known of the town at this time, but after Edward I conquered Wales, he had a survey made of Merioneth between 1285 and 1310, rather similar to Domesday Book, in which there is a very full description of Dolgellau. The people living there were tenants of the Crown and were of two different kinds, Welshmen and 'foreigners', that is Englishmen and Irishmen. The accounts show that, to a great extent, the burden of agriculture fell on the foreigners, and that the Welsh were primarily cattle breeders, large herds being kept round Dolgellau and grazed on Cae Marian, a field near the river Wnion, where 600 years later, Welsh cattle were shod before starting on their long journey to the markets of Kent and Essex. Edward I spent some time in

Merioneth while the survey was being carried out, and in May 1295 he received the homage of local tribal chieftains in Dolgellau. But he never made it a Borough and it is one of the very few county towns which has never returned a member of Parliament.

Walter de Manny, a vicecome of the Shire of Merioneth in the reign of Edward III, established fairs and markets; tolls which came to about 3½ per cent of the selling prices of the goods were levied on every horse, ox and cow, on every horseload of butter, oats and honey, and each bale of wool. The uneasy peace which existed between England and Wales for many years after the Statutes of Rhuddlan, 1285, was rudely shattered in 1401 when Owain Glyndwr raised the standard of revolt in Merioneth. In a fierce battle that followed, the English under the command of Hotspur, the King's Governor for North Wales, were forced to retreat. It was from Dolgellau that Glyndwr sent letters to the Kings of Scotland and France, asking for help and pleading the justice of his fight against English usurpation, signing himself *'Owinus, Dei gratia princeps Walliae datum apud Dolgeuelli 10 mie mensis Maii, MCCCC quarto.'*

Glyndwr dreamed of a Wales free from English domination, with two universities, one in the North and the other in the South, and of a Welsh church completely independent of Canterbury. But this was not to be; Glyndwr's armies were defeated and he vanished as completely as his dreams, for it is not known even when he died. He is still called to mind in Dolgellau by an ironmonger's shop named Parliament House, built on the site of the place where he stayed and held meetings with his councillors. The original Parliament House was taken down in 1883 and rebuilt in Newtown, Montgomeryshire.

During the Civil War, Sir William Vaughan levied a toll of £140 on the wool merchants to raise money for the King. For many hundreds of years, from the time when the Cistercian monks came to Merioneth in 1189 and by better methods of sheep breeding, vastly improved the standard of Welsh wool, Dolgellau was connected with the wool trade; indeed, at one time, with the exception of Llanidloes and Newtown, it was the largest wool-producing town in Wales. The weavers were so quick and accurate that many other towns tried to lure them away, and higher prices were paid for Dolgellau wool than for any other. The manufacture in Dolgellau of a kind of coarse woollen cloth, or flannel, called 'webs' is of remote origin, and is mentioned in Acts of Parliament in James I's reign; there were orders for its regulation from the Privy Council of Charles I. To encourage the woollen trade a law was passed in 1678 making it obligatory for only woollen shrouds to be used, and in a Register of Dolgellau Parish Church (1678-1708) entries of burials are supported by affidavits, signed by the Rector, stating that this law had been carried out.

In the later eighteenth century, in or around the town there were many fulling mills where cloth made on handlooms was taken to be thickened by being beaten with huge water-driven hammers. At one time most of the webs went to Shrewsbury, but later a substantial export trade developed, 25,000yd going abroad annually. This was due to the flourishing craft of shipbuilding which grew up in the Mawddach, which a few miles below Dolgellau broadened out into an estuary of surpassing beauty. Gazing over the now placid deserted waters, it seems almost impossible that once the estuary was a busy inland waterway of prime importance to Dolgellau and to the outside world. By way of Barmouth and Liverpool, Dolgellau woollens, known as frieze of Cambria, went to Charlestown in South Carolina to clothe the slaves; Spanish colonists wore Dolgellau woollens, the British army fought in them, and they were exported to Africa and a number of European countries, including Germany and Holland. The roads were in so bad a state that most of the woollen goods were taken by packhorse to the sixteenth-century bridge just below Llanelltyd, and loaded into sloops which sailed down the estuary to Barmouth, then a busy sea port, and thence to Liverpool.

During the eighteenth and nineteenth centuries the building of some kind of ship, from rowing boats to a brigantine, was going on in almost every creek and inlet along the Mawddach estuary. It was considered lucky, here as elsewhere, for a woman to launch the ships — which were nearly always given women's names; a religious service was generally held at the launching ceremony, followed by feasting and revelry.

An important shipyard, one in great demand, was at Maes-y-garnedd, a little creek below Llanelltyd and about six miles from Barmouth. Here crafts such as smacks were built. Thomas Pennant in his *Tours in Wales* mentioned with interest that he saw 'a small sloop, ready to be launched'. Maes-y-garnedd was also a distributing point for goods for people living in the hinterland of the county. All kinds of commodities were brought by barges and sailing boats from Barmouth to Maes-y-garnedd, including beans, flour, oatmeal, rye, rice, wheat, soap, candles, salt, coal, timber, bark and wine. At Maes-y-garnedd they were unloaded and taken to their destination by packhorses. Further down the Mawddach estuary, in a creek at Penmaenpool, much bigger ships like large two-masted schooners (and at least one brigantine) were built. Glandwr was another creek where little boats brought stores from large coastal ships which put in at Barmouth. A great deal of cargo consisted of seaweed, which at that time was a form of manure extensively used by farmers living fairly near the sea. But the coming of the railway gradually extinguished the Mawddach shipbuilding craft, and the discovery that Merioneth oak very easily developed dry rot also perhaps hastened its demise.

But the Dolgellau woollen industry continued to flourish. A writer in 1833 said that 1,400 people were employed in the flannel industry and the number of pieces made annually amounted to 30,000, averaging 110 yards each. 'The warp is fleece wool of the county, the woof is a mixture containing about half and sometimes a third of lambs' wool.' In 1873 a visitor wrote, 'No visitor should leave Dolgellau without seeing the primitive way flannels and tweeds are made. The price at which the tweeds are sold is something ridiculous, I bought stuff for a complete suit of what was termed "Wynnstay fishing cloth" for 16s 10d and the cloth has this merit to the economical, when it begins to look shabby you may turn your coat, and your outward appearance will be improved.'

At one time Dolgellau also had a flourishing tanning industry — there were six skinners' yards and three tanneries, and about 100,000 local lamb skins, as well as many kid skins, were sent to Worcester and Chester every year, and some to London. The tanneries were of two kinds: the heavy leather that tanned hides and the light leather which dealt with sheepskins. One of the oldest of the second kind was founded nearly a hundred years ago by Robert Meredith. The firm closed the tanning side of the business in 1939, but continued first as wool merchants and fellmongers for a number of years, and now as fellmongers. The Merediths have been in business in Dolgellau for four generations.

In 1965 I was fortunate enough to be shown round the business. In those days local farmers brought in their wool in large sacks and stored them in a huge stone building, round the sides of which were divisions called 'bins' where the wool was placed when it had been graded; an extremely skilled job for there were so many different gradings of wool. The prices ranged from Grade I at 52½d per pound and picked Crossbred at 66d a pound, to 35d a pound for Greasy

Turbary Welsh. When the wool had been graded it was pushed through an aperture in the floor to a metal container at one end of which a machine called a 'ram' squeezed the wool tightly together. It was then put in packs and sent to Bradford.

David Meredith & Sons Ltd are now engaged as fellmongers, dealing exclusively with sheepskins. All round the yard are piles of skins awaiting treatment. First they are roughly treated with salt to prevent them decomposing and then to soften them they are soaked in enormous concrete baths. When I first visited Meredith's, men were painting the softened skins with huge brushes soaked in a green mixture composed of sodium, phosphate, lime and water. By this method 150 to 180 skins could be treated every day — now use of a spray has increased the number from 800 to 1000.

After the fleeces have been hung up to dry for a time the wool can be pulled off perfectly easily by hand. The wool, once separated from the skin, is put into a kind of outsize spin drier, and the skins are soaked again in a 'paddle', eventually going to a tannery at Heywood near Manchester to be made into leather.

During the summer the main square of Dolgellau and the streets leading directly to it are crowded with tourists, but five minutes' walk down a narrow, twisting lane leads you to an entirely different world, where another ancient craft is still being practised, to Pop t'r Lawnt where bread has been baked for over two hundred years. There you will find Dafydd Ellis Rowlands, one of those splendidly individualistic Welshmen. In the little bakery you step back into the past, for there bread is still made in the old traditional way. Mr Rowlands is certainly the last master-baker in Merioneth, and probably in a much wider area, who makes his bread and a variety of buns entirely by hand and bakes them in old-fashioned coke-fired ovens. Kneading the dough in the correct way is a vital part of successful bread making. While I waited with Mr Rowlands for a batch of bread to be taken out of the oven, he told me something of his life.

Taught by his father, he began baking when he was twelve and he had been doing it ever since. Years ago he shared a hand cart with an upholsterer, who used it in the mornings, with its top off, to wheel sofas and chairs to his workshop. Mr Rowlands had it in the afternoons, put the top back again and delivered his loaves in it. He makes about 100 loaves a day and how great is the variety can be seen by the tins for the loaves, which are of every conceivable size. The big ovens are fired by coke, which when Mr Rolands first used it cost 4½d a cwt. These days he uses a comparatively small metal implement for getting the bread out of the ovens but behind him can be seen the huge 'peels' which he used in the past. He has one quite small oven in which buns are left to rise, or as he phrased it 'put the wind in them'. I have not tasted such bread since my mother used to make it, over fifty years ago.

The bakery is far more than just a shop; it is also a social club where people of all ages drop in to chat, or to discuss a wide variety of topics — religion, politics and local news — but above all, music. For besides being a master-baker, Mr Rowlands, or Dafydd Wyn to give him his bardic name, is an accomplished conductor, like his father before him. A born musician with little formal training, he has been conducting choirs for over fifty years. He started his career as a conductor in 1924, with a mixed choir from the Dolgellau Tabernacle Chapel, which became an all male choir in 1933. During World War II it raised over £7,000 for various charities. The choir's list of achievements is impressive. At one National Eisteddfod they won the Perpetual Challenge Cup for male voices; they were first one year at the Butlin Camp Annual Eisteddfod, and another year they entered fourteen competitions and gained eleven firsts, two seconds and one third prize. At the present time, the choir has fifty-six members, many of whom travel nearly fifty miles to attend the weekly practices in Dolgellau. (Since writing this, Mr Rowlands has retired and the bakery closed).

For hundreds of years Dolgellau has attracted visitors. Some of them in the seventeenth and eighteenth centuries were rather critical of the little town, complaining that every entrance was barred by a turnpike, that the streets were irregular and narrow, the houses small and ill-lit, but during the first part of the nineteenth century the town centre was vastly improved by Sir Robert Williames Vaughan of Nannau. Modern Dolgellau with its narrow streets, and little squares, has a charm all of its own, and so have the picturesque old cottages, the fine seventeenth-century bridge spanning the Wnion, the old hotels, the various shops and offices, for they are all built of large, grey stones, enduring and massive as the five peaks of Cader Idris which tower for nearly 3,000 ft behind the town like a rampart.

Richard Fenton, writing in August 1808, remarked that 'The Masonry of Dolgelley merits particular notice. From time immemorial they have been built with very large stones, even to the top, lifting the Stones of the work from towards the middle course with an immense machine which takes above a day to erect, and worked by two men, every stone being of such weight as to require a Lever of that vast power.'

People used to ride up Cader and at one time as many as forty to fifty sturdy Welsh ponies were kept at one hotel for this purpose, and another hotel advertised 'ponies and guides, fixed, moderate prices'. One of the most famous guides was Robert Edwards, who at the age of eighty-four used to hand out printed circulars to visitors in which he described himself — among other things — as 'being by chance made a glover, by genious a fly dresser and angler, and now, by the all-divine assistance, conductor to and over the most tremendous mountain Cader Idris.'

One of the most interesting old hostelries in Dolgellau is

116

the Golden Lion Royal Hotel, for round it for several centuries revolved the social life of the town and neighbourhood, and some extremely curious incidents have taken place within its granite walls and those of its predecessor. The original coaching inn which stood on the site of the present building was called Plas Isa, and was described as 'the chief hotel in Dolgelley and as comfortable as most hotels in small towns during the eighteenth century.' When Thomas Pennant stayed there he was very enthusiastic about the excellence of the harpist. It was there for many years that the judge had his lodgings when the Assizes were held at Dolgellau. The magnificent grey stone building we know today as the Golden Lion Royal Hotel was built on the site of the old hostelry by Sir Robert.

It was owing to the quickness of Catherine Evans, a barmaid at the hotel, that a clever forger, John Greenwood, was caught. One morning in February 1813, a stranger asked Catherine for a negus — a glass of warm, spiced wine — which he paid for with a £5 note, and then left. Feeling suspicious about the note, Catherine at once showed it to the proprietor who, guessing it was spurious, ran out of the hotel after the stranger. He was fortunate enough to meet Colonel Price of Rhiwlas, Bala, a County Justice, riding down the main street; he immediately went off in pursuit of Greenwood. Colonel Price ran him to earth at an inn in Trawsfynydd, some twelve miles from Dolgellau, and on being stripped, quantities of forged notes were found on him. He was duly hanged at Dolgellau in May 1813, before a large crowd, one of the last public executions.

About the middle of the nineteenth century a couple who shall be nameless — their families are still well-known in the district — decided to have a runaway marriage, for she was an heiress and her family disapproved of her penniless suitor. After a secret wedding ceremony at Llanfachreth Church, the bridal pair drove to the Golden Lion. With the air of a conquering hero the bridegroom called out, 'Whisky for me, wine for the lady,' and smacking down a sovereign added, 'I have married £6,000 of these gold coins today!'

Dolgellau parish church, though not an old building, has its interest. During the eleventh century a great revival of the cult of the Virgin Mary took place in Wales, and the first documentary evidence of a church dedicated to her in Dolgellau is found in the Norwich Taxatio of 1255; Camden, in the sixteenth century, speaks of the outer structure merely as 'seemly'. A print dated 1662 shows the ancient church; there was no belfry, so the bells hung in an adjacent yew tree. The old church was demolished in 1716, though not till the new structure was completed. The only relic from it is a fine recumbent effigy of Meurig ap Ynyr Vychan who lived in the twelfth century, and it shows the fierce old warrior, clad in close mail, his sword in his hand, his dog at his feet. He was Lord of Nannau and was renowned for his hospitality, and probably he was also a pious man, for a surviving deed records Robert, Abbot Bardsey, receiving under 'the spritual protection of the Abbey, Meurig Vychan of Nanney, his wife, his parents and issue.'

Writing in 1818, Richard Fenton said that the church 'has this great singularity that it has no Pews, only Forms of Wood, with the Names of the different proprietors painted on the back; . . . producing a very awkward effect, but certainly, by being open, they are more likely to induce those who sit in them to deport themselves more decently than when they are boarded up in high-sided Pews.' In the present church, the roof of the nave is supported by eight enormous wooden pillars which were drawn, long ago, by oxen over the precipitous pass from Dinas Mawddwy, some ten miles away. It used to be the custom before a coffin was committed to the ground to unscrew the brass plates and place them on the wooden pillars, but unfortunately these curious memorials have all been taken down.

Llew Evans, farmer, musician and folklorist, at the organ in his home

Mari Jones (*right*), post woman and farmer, with her sister Annie

(*above*) 'Hughie
Ffriddgoch' with his hay
sleigh
(*right*) St Derfel's wooden
horse
(*below right*) Pennant
Melangell Church

In 1721 the Reverend Ellis Lewis left a sum of money for a peal of eight bells, some of which were used for unusual customs. The first, second and third bells were chimed for Divine Service, number four was the curfew, and number five was rung for a fire. Number six was the funeral bell, three sets of three strokes to be tolled for a man, three sets of two strokes for a woman and three single strokes for a child. After this the knell informed parishioners that a public funeral would take place the next day. The seventh bell was called *'y gloch goll'* and was sounded if a climber was missing on Cader Idris, so that people could gather in the square and search parties be organised. The eighth bell was the Communion one. If a funeral was going through the parish, the passing bell, the largest, was sounded. The smallest bell, the treble, was rung to give the date of the month just before the curfew was sounded each evening at nine o'clock. Sad to say, for lack of ringers the bells are seldom heard now.

The modern Roman Catholic Church in Dolgellau — dedicated to Our Lady of Sorrows — is of special interest for it is unlikely that ever again will a stone building of its size, designed and built by local craftsmen from local materials, be erected. There was a small, inadequate Roman Catholic place of worship, but Father Scalpell, the Priest in Charge, yearned for a far better building, though this seemed an impossible dream. The parish extended about 12 miles around Dolgellau, and his only means of transport was a bicycle, which he rode until such exertion was too much for him; then he walked instead. There were few Catholics in the neighbourhood, fewer still who were wealthy, the average Sunday collections varying from 5s to 8s. Father Scalpell wrote more than 25,000 letters to people in every part of the world, trying to raise money for a church. But the years went by and there seemed no hope of the dream coming true.

Then one day, after Mass, when Father Scalpell had been appealing for funds, a stranger remained behind and asked him how much he still required to build another church and the priest named a five-figure sum. Taking Father Scalpell's name and address and refusing to give his own, the stranger said he would give him the money and then left. No one was more surprised than Father Scalpell when, not long afterwards, he received a letter from a solicitor saying that a client of his would give him the money for his church on two conditions: he would always remain anonymous and the church must be a fine building, harmonising with its austere, mountainous surroundings. The conditions were fulfilled.

Work started in 1963 and the Norman-style church took about four years to finish at a cost of around £44,000. All the stone used was from either Caernarvonshire or Merioneth and was obtained from four different quarries so that there should be a variation in colouring. The architect, Maurice Pritchard, the building contractors, John Evans and Sons, the masons and the craftsmen, were all local men.

Dolgellau is more isolated now than it was over a hundred years ago, for the railway line to Bala and Ruabon, which was opened in 1868, closed in 1964, leaving the town without any rail link. Many colourful characters travelled on the line, some of whom I was lucky enough to meet. I think of the shepherd who had very little English but a profound knowledge of Welsh poets and the intricacies of Welsh poetry with its extremely complicated rules concerning metre; I remember the old salmon poacher who nearly fell out of the carriage window in his excitement as he pointed out to me the exact places in the river Wnion that ran close to the line where his youthful and illicit exploits had occurred.

I think too of the retired engine driver who held me enthralled with stories of the railway sixty years ago. In those days the trains would stop anywhere between stations to pick up a farmer, and in return, a few days later, neatly labelled gifts of butter or eggs or perhaps a rabbit, would be hung on the walls by the line for co-operative guards and engine drivers.

One of the oddest characters to travel on the line was Dai Jones, who many of my friends remember. His work as a shepherd often took him miles away from his home to such desolate and uninhabited country that he had no opportunity to spend money. He was sometimes up there for as long as six months, so when he eventually came home he had a considerable sum of wages to collect from his employer. This he quickly got rid of in a truly spectacular way. He would hire a special train which took him in solitary splendour from Dolgellau to Bala, some 18 miles distant, where he had such a wonderful time spending his substance in riotous living that when he returned home it had to be on foot.

Sir Robert Vaughan of Garthmaelan, a well-known figure in Dolgellau when I was a child, farmed extensively, but one of his chief interests was the Great Western Railway of which he was a director. His English wife never felt really happy in Wales, so he bought her a farm in England. Every year they spent a couple of months there, migrating thither like the patriarchs of old, for Sir Robert took literally all his livestock with him by train — cattle, sheep, goats, as well as numerous dogs and thirty cats. During a railway strike he drove a train. On one occasion he saw that the level-crossing gates were closed against him, so he put on steam, crashed through them and brought the train to safety on the other side.

The railway has gone for ever, but the road that in many places runs beside it passes through superb scenery and near some interesting old cottages. One of the toll gates which those travelling to Dolgellau in the seventeenth and eighteenth centuries disliked so much is situated just a few miles from Dolgellau along the road. It is a pretty little grey stone cottage and a couple of years ago when a gable was being repaired, a large slate was taken from the roof and on one side was found a list of the tolls imposed until they were abolished in 1875. The slate has now been placed on the front of the house and reads:

123

Every Horse or other Beast drawing any Coach, Chariot, Chair with four wheels 6d., For every other Horse or Beast drawing any wagon with four or two wheels 4d., For every Horse or other Beast laden or unladen and not drawing 1½d; For every drove of Oxen, Cows or Meat Cattle per score and so in proportion for any less number 10d. For every drove of Calves, Hogs, Sheep, Lambs or Goats per score and so in proportion for any less number 5d.

The road from Dolgellau to Bala winds up the steep Pass of Garneddwen, through a wild and uninhabited region where on either side grim mountains tower up for nearly 3,000 ft; in the valley below, the river Wnion foams and roars over its rocky bed. Fortunately for travellers in this desolate part of Merioneth, for over 200 years there has been an inn by the side of the road halfway up the bleak pass. The earliest one about which anything is known was described by a traveller as 'a poor Hovel', but this was rebuilt in 1789 by Sir Robert Hywel Vaughan of Nannau. It was called Hen Dafarn Drws-y-nant, 'The Old Tavern at the Gateway of the Stream', and it looks much the same today as it did when painted by Moses Griffiths in the eighteenth century.

The inn became an important meeting-place for all kinds of people. At one time it was a posting stage; valuable sheep and wool sales were held there till 1935; while during the latter part of the eighteenth century, a society composed of Welsh poets and men of letters met there every month on the first Thursday before the full moon, to discuss the arts and drink the ale for which the inn was famous. The Moon Society was founded by Rhys Jones of Blaenau, in the parish of Llanfachreth, poet and antiquary, who will always be remembered for his *Gorchestion Beirdd Cymru*. Another famous visitor was Lewis Morris of Anglesey. In the course of his many journeys through Wales to inspect lead mines, he often stayed at Hen Dafarn. He was a poet of distinction, and it was in the garden opposite the old house that he composed his beautiful song, *Caniad y Gog i*

Merionydd — 'The Cuckoo's Homage to Merioneth'. The poet has died long since, the garden where he wrote his poem is now a car park, but he is still remembered at the inn, for in a tiny recess on the right-hand side of the fireplace in the kitchen is a slate plaque inscribed with his name.

Very strict rules governed the running of the tavern. In a recognizance granted to 'William Jones of Drws-y-nant, Innkeeper' on 7 October 1817, he was empowered 'to keep a Common Inn, Ale-house, or Victualling-house, for ONE YEAR from the TWENTYNINTH of this present MONTH of SEPTEMBER, in the House where he now dwelleth at Drws-y-nant aforesaid'. But it was only on condition that 'he the said William Jones shall keep and maintain in good Order and Rule and suffer no Disorders of unlawful Games in his said House, nor in any Outhouse, Yard, Garden or Premises during the said Term. . . .'

In 1868, the navvies working on the extension of the railway line from Bala to Dolgellau used to pour into the Old Tavern for drinks. Attached to the inn was a lean-to, which has since been demolished, called *Cegin-y-Gwyddelod*, 'The Irishmen's Kitchen'. This was set aside for the Irish navvies, for the Welsh refused to drink with them.

In 1903, life changed radically at the old tavern. Robert Roberts had just married and wanted somewhere to live. He was greatly attracted by the inn and the farm which went with it, but he and his wife were strict teetotallers. This difficulty was solved by the owner, General Vaughan of Nannau, agreeing to take away the licence. The inn was renamed the Hywel Dda — Hywel the Good — in honour of the great tenth-century Welsh king, the lawgiver, and mineral waters and tea replaced the beer for which the inn had been famous for so many years. The following summary of the detailed inventory drawn up when Robert Roberts took over gives an interesting idea of values in 1903.

Crops, cattle, farm implements, harness, etc.	£143	7s	6d
400 sheep at 22s 9d per head	455	0s	0d
Barn, fences, etc.	45	0s	0d
Contents of house	26	13s	0d
	£670	0s	6d

The Hywel Dda became so popular and busy that soon after the Roberts married, their young niece, now Mrs Thomas, came to help them, and she recalls fascinating details of their life. It seems astonishing that in those pre-motoring days so many people came from so far away to such a lonely inn. 'No bed and breakfast in those days between Bala and Dolgellau. People from all parts were coming by train to climb the Arans' — desolate mountains near the Hywel Dda which rose for nearly 3,000 feet. 'They called for a drink in the morning, a cup of tea and sandwiches at night before going back by train. Many people from overseas. Every summer before the first world war we had many students from German Colleges going up the Arans . . . they went everywhere in Wales. They were so nice we never thought they would fight us.'

There were also numbers of cycling parties. 'One of them came in and gave me a note; they were deaf and dumb, wanting tea, ham and eggs, it was very touching to see them chatting with their hands. They did enjoy themselves. Another time, one lovely summer evening an Officer with about 30 Horse Guards came in, all wanting supper and breakfast. Luckily we had everything except bread, but kind neighbours helped us. The men slept with their horses.' Mrs Thomas goes on to say 'There were a lot of High Class people coming in their carriages and pairs — large shooting parties in August too.' Charges were: Bed 2s. 0d; breakfast 1s 6d; tea 6d. to 10d; suppers 10d to 1s.

As well as the inn, there was the farm to be looked after, with some 400 sheep, 8 cows, and bullocks and calves, as well as poultry and pigs. As regards food, the Roberts were almost self-supporting. Every year four pigs were killed to provide bacon and ham for the visitors; about 10 lb of butter was made every churning day; all the bread was baked in a huge brick oven. 'We used to make porridge from our own corn, the miller used to dry it for us; we had our own vegetables too.'

In the summer Mrs Thomas had to walk up the mountain to milk the cows — in hot weather they were difficult to find as they sheltered among the bracken from the heat. 'I used to milk them myself and carry the milk down on my back about a quarter of a mile.' Sheep-shearing was a specially busy time, for large breakfasts had to be provided for the men who got up at four in the morning to gather the sheep from high up on the mountain sheep walks. The sheep were washed in the river below the Hywel Dda to clean them before shearing. 'We used to make fires and sandwiches and cakes and bara brith' — a kind of currant loaf. 'The night before the house was full, we only had a few hours sleep, we had to prepare for three days before, making bread and cakes in the big oven and a round of beef.'

A hard life indeed but Mrs Thomas says it was a happy one. During the long, cold winters, even in the most isolated farms among the mountains, wonderful parties were given and people walked many miles to attend them. 'We had lovely suppers; fowls or geese with apple sauce or bread sauce and stuffing, all sorts of vegetables and plum pudding. Then we played cards or games, till about 1 o'clock [in the morning] we had a cup of tea with trifles and all kinds of cakes.' On one occasion the plum pudding had been put in the wash house outside to boil, but when someone went to fetch it and took the lid off the copper, only an old boot was found. Some boys had stolen it.

After the Roberts left, the Hywel Dda changed hands several times. Now again it is a licensed inn; essential restorations and repairs have been so skilfully carried out that the character of the fine old house has not been spoiled.

In the desolate country beyond the Hywel Dda there seem

to be few signs of human habitation, yet for those who know where to look some tiny stone cottages can still be found which though they seem entirely commonplace, have a history linked with the remote past when Wales was an independent kingdom, governed by tribal laws of great antiquity. By these laws, members of the tribe had the right to a certain amount of land, and though in the end Wales was conquered by England and the tribal system perished, hunger for land remained a dominant characteristic of the Welsh.

As the centuries passed and the system of land enclosure increased, this hunger for land became more and more difficult to satisfy, so very gradually the custom of building *tai-un-nos*, that is literally 'one-night houses', became widespread. A piece of waste land in a remote place was chosen and a dwelling place with a roof on it and smoke coming out of the chimney had to be built between sunset and sunrise. The materials could be collected beforehand and any number of people could help, but the actual building had to be done within the prescribed hours. These little houses, which were also rather charmingly called 'morning surprises', were built of large stones, with turf roofs. The amount of land the builder of a *ty-un-nos* claimed was determined by his throwing an axe from the door of his cottage to the various points of the compass. A hedge was planted along this line and the land within was considered his.

A *ty-un-nos* was only freehold if it escaped detection by the owner of the land for twelve years, that is until the Statute of Limitation had expired, and this happened oftener than might be supposed, for the one-night houses were generally built in very inaccessible places. I know of one which was built some 1,600 feet up the precipitous slopes of Rhobell mountain in Merioneth, in such a lonely place that not even a cart track runs up to it. The idea that freehold rights were automatically acquired by building a one-night house was erroneous in point of law, but was widespread throughout Wales and greatly encouraged encroachment. The origins of the belief are obscure. The Royal Commission on Land in Wales and Monmouth, published in 1896, says, 'Among the ancient Welsh laws can be found the statement, "Three necessary things for a man — roof-tree, roof-forks, and wattling; and he is free to cut them in such wild woods as he may please." This may point to this usage as being recognised before the Conquest and the description recalls the actual appearance of some of the oldest *tai-un-nos*. If there was in early times an inherent right in every free member of the community to have some allotment of the land of the tribe or clan, it is not difficult to see how such a right might develop into the notion of the *ty-un-nos*.'

Whatever the origins of the custom, it is clear from the evidence collected by the Royal Commission that squatting and encroachment had gone on for a great number of years unchecked and seem to some extent to have been sanctioned by public opinion. The practice was most prevalent in the eighteenth century and in the first part of the nineteenth century, but after that time the housing shortage and the hunger for land diminished, as the rural population of Wales began to drift away to the growing industrial centres of England. In some ways the squatters did no harm; indeed they reclaimed and greatly improved land which would otherwise have remained derelict. But as time went on, encroachments were so numerous that they became a nuisance. One nobleman had no less than 800 on his estate; a large landowner in Cardiganshire told the Royal Commission that out of his 500 cottage tenants, only 40 paid rack rent, and in Caernarvonshire, near the slate quarries in a parish of 9,516 acres, there were 141 encroachments containing 337 acres which supported 81 cows and 683 people.

The quarrymen used to work on moonlight nights, levelling the ground, reclaiming the land and carting stones to build houses. The land had originally belonged to the Crown and when an attempt was made to raise the rent of the land and cottages, the squatters resisted strenuously. A protest meeting was held by the London Welshmen on 19 April 1827, a fighting fund was raised, three Welsh solicitors in London took up the case and Parliament was petitioned. The squatters won, and to show their gratitude they sent several casks of home-brewed ale to their London supporters.

Many of the squatters were not content with the first piece of land they had taken; gradually more and more land was brought under cultivation and the first tiny cottages were much enlarged and improved, but great resentment was felt by those who were not freeholders when their rent was raised. A letter in the *Herald Cymraeg* complains: 'I know a man of 75 who has led a steady and industrious life all his days, he obeyed the laws of his country and the commandments of his God, he erected a house and cultivated three acres of Crown land, and he thought that would afford him shelter from want in his old days. All his labours were in vain; the great, powerful, opulent Government of a Christian Britain took away all his means, for he has to pay £4 a year to the Government for value created by his own labour.'

Though no new one-night houses have been built within living memory and most of the old ones are now in ruins, there are just a few left which until quite recently were still inhabited. A few years ago I called on two friends who lived in *tai-un-nos* and only died last year. The cottages are situated in a desolate, almost treeless part of Merioneth, where the wind is always blowing, where many streams flow and where a great mountain stretches its grim heights upwards for nearly 3,000 ft. It was a long walk up a steep, stony track winding through heather to Mrs Wilson's cottage, Rhos Dylluan, 'The Owls' Moor'. Crouched among great grey boulders and long grass and sheltered by a few twisted trees, it consists of one room up and one room down, with a tiny scullery at the back built on about seventy years ago.

Mrs Wilson told me about the cottage which had been enlarged and rebuilt round a *ty-un-nos* a few years before it was given to her mother as a wedding present about 1880. It had been freehold then, but at the beginning of this century the landowner offered to do certain repairs and renew the roof, in return for the payment of a small yearly rent. Unsuspectingly Mrs Wilson's father agreed, and so the freehold was lost. Except for her brief married life, Mrs Wilson had always lived at Rhos Dylluan. She was one of nine children, but when I visited her she was alone, except for three petted tabby cats, and aged eighty-seven. There are no modern conveniences in the cottage but it was only shortly before she died that she could be induced to leave. She carried all her water from a nearby stream, a task she found easier than drawing up water from the deep well under the kitchen floor, which had been used when she was a child. In very hot weather, crocks of butter were kept in the well. Mrs Wilson was far too busy to feel the need of television or radio; her spare time was spent writing articles and poems for various Welsh papers, and in reading.

About a mile from Rhos Dylluan, across the slopes of the mountain, is another little cottage. It was rebuilt around the original *ty-un-nos* in 1895 by the grandfather of a Mr Roberts, who lived there all his life until he died a short while ago. He was well over eighty but thought nothing of walking many miles to the nearest little village to do his shopping. He was perfectly content living alone.

Eventually the few one-night houses that are still inhabited will be empty, for no one will want to live in such lonely places where even in summer time few people pass and during the long winter nights the only sounds are the owls hooting over the waste lands, the roaring of many waters and the wind from the barren mountain tops howling in the darkness. So at last a unique way of life will come to an end and another fascinating link with the Wales of long ago will be broken.

131

As the road approaches Bala, the great rocky promontory called Carn Dochan rears up as though still commanding the surrounding countryside, for here the Romans once mined for gold and in the twelfth century the Welsh built a small fort. According to legend, a golden cauldron and a golden harp are buried under the floor of the fort and if they are disturbed, the heavens will be rent by thunder and lightning. A Roman road ran obliquely through Wales from Chester to the Mawddach Estuary. To protect this road in the Bala area, about the year 78 AD, not far from Carn Dochan, the Romans built a fort at Caer Gai, high above the lake in a commanding position looking south. It occupied some 425 square feet and its defences consisted of a ditch in front of a wall, backed by an earth bank. It was probably garrisoned by the first Cohort of the Nervians and occupied till 150 AD. A fine mansion now stands on the site of the Roman fort.

Bala is a small town, its population under 2,000, but it has a fascinating and varied history stretching far back into the past; it is the centre of one of the most truly 'Welsh' districts still left in Wales and is set in a fertile valley of great beauty. There is evidence to suggest that there may have been lake dwellings at the northern end of the lake, the Romans passed that way, while in the town itself there is still the castle mound, *Tomen-y-Bala*, built by the Norman invaders during the twelfth century and destroyed by the Welsh in 1201. The real history of Bala began when it was founded as a small commercial centre about 1310 by Roger de Mortimer, the Justiciar of North Wales from 1307 to 1314. The land was marked out into burgages and there seems to have been quite a colony of English settlers, probably put there to keep the Welsh in subjection. This object was apparently not achieved, for Bala was noted for its lawlessness and a charter granted by Edward III, one of four given by various English monarchs, refers to the fact that in the district 'robbers and marauders assemble together, and that numerous crimes and depredations are committed on travellers.'

Bala was made a Borough in 1324 and came under the jurisdiction of Harlech Castle. Apparently 'the inhabitants of mediaeval Bala were few. They were chiefly occupied in agriculture and pastoral pursuits. some of the townsmen concurrently farmed the grinding mills at Pennaran and Bala.' Before long Bala became one of the foremost markets in North Wales and actually paid more to the Crown in commercial tolls than in rents of land.

Though this prosperity seems to have declined for a time, during the sixteenth and seventeenth centuries, the knitting and woollen industry gradually developed to such an extent that a writer in 1812 said 'Bala is noted for its vast trade in woollen stockings, gloves and caps called Welsh Wigs.' These were made from the hair of wild goats, which in those days roamed over the Merioneth mountains in considerable numbers and were apparently thought very highly of in London society. Each week knitted goods valued from £200 to £500 were sold, an astonishing figure in so sparsely populated an area, but the women of Bala were supposed to be able to turn every 1d worth of wool into 1s. In and around Bala, women and children could be seen walking along the roads knitting during the summer months; when winter came they assembled at each others' houses where singing, story-telling and harp music helped to speed their needles. The stockings, which were bright red for children, blue or grey for men and black for women, were 'so distinguished for their softness of texture that they were specially recommended by the medical faculty'. The men also knitted and one man, famed for his speed, was a well-known preacher who always knitted when composing his sermons.

By 1830, 32,000 dozen pairs of stockings, 10,000 dozen pairs of socks and 5,500 dozen pairs of gloves were made annually. Another source of income was the sale of butter; at one time about three tons a week were sent in firkins during the summer to Chester, Holywell, Denbigh and other markets. Bala was also a great centre for the sale of Welsh ponies called merlins, which lived on the mountains in large numbers, completely wild. Catching them was a hazardous task but one which the farmers enjoyed.

But Bala was not only concerned with the making of money. It was also a religious and cultural centre. Indeed it has been called 'the Athens of Wales' and at one time could be said to have been the centre of nonconformity in Wales. There stood the Welsh Calvinistic Methodist and the Independent Colleges, from whence for many years Wales received an unbroken succession of eloquent and dedicated preachers. Hard by the Calvinistic Chapel stands the statue of Thomas Charles, 1755-1814, an indefatigable promoter of Sunday Schools and circulating Church Schools; the man who had the vision to realise that what was greatly needed in Wales was a cheap and plentiful supply of Bibles written in Welsh, so that all could study the word of God. This was brought home to him when a child, Mary Jones, walked some thirty miles from Llanfihangel-yn-Pennant over the mountains to Bala to get a Welsh Bible, and Charles had to give her his own — no other was available. He was so moved that he laid the facts before the Religious Tract Society of which he was a member, and as a direct result the British and Foreign Bible Society was formed. One of its first tasks was the production of a Welsh Bible under the editorship of Thomas Charles.

For hundreds of years Welshmen dreamed of a Welsh settlement beyond the seas, completely free from English domination. By the middle of the nineteenth century, agrarian and religious troubles brought matters to a head. Michael Daniel Jones of Bala was one of the prime movers in the negotiations with the Argentine Government which finally resulted in the founding of the Welsh Settlement in Patagonia in 1865 and many of the original settlers came from the Bala area.

8

Animals and Saints
in Welsh Folklore

Religion has been a passionately important part of Welsh life and ancient churches and more modern nonconformist chapels stand in every corner of the countryside. The feeling of mystery which haunts so much of beautiful Merioneth also pervades many of the ancient churches. Many have queer stories associated with them that date back to pre-christian times; the austere grey walls of others hide surprising treasures. Llandderfel is one of these: its rather uninteresting exterior gives no hint that it housed an ancient relic which the Royal Commission on Ancient Monuments in Wales described in 1913 as 'one of the most interesting objects of mediaeval archaeology in the country'. The story goes back many centuries.

The church is dedicated to Derfel Gadarn, a sixth-century saint of whom little is known except that he founded this church in Merioneth and that he became abbot of the famous monastery on Bardsey Island. He is said to have been a great warrior in his youth and to have fought in the battle of Camlan, in 537. Many centuries ago, no one now knows when, a huge wooden effigy was made of him, mounted on a horse, which was held in such veneration that hundreds of people used to come and visit it, bringing offerings of cattle, horses and money. Every Easter Tuesday it was carried in procession and set up on Bryn Sant — the Saint's Hill — near where the Rectory now stands, a great gathering forming round it.

135

Unfortunately these proceedings filled the protestant Dr Ellis Price, Commissary General for the Diocese of St Asaph, with horror, and he wrote in April 1538 to the authorities in London that 'the inncocente people hath been sore alured and entised to worshipe the said Image, in so muche that there is a common saying as yet amongst them, that who so ever will offer anie thing to the saide Image of Darfelgadarn, he hethe power to fetche hym or them that so offers oute of hell where they be damned.' On the saint's festival, Dr Price estimated that some 500 to 600 people assembled to venerate the image. In spite of the angry protests of the people and an offer of £40 to save the image, it was wrenched off the wooden horse and taken to London. Just at this time, Father Forest, a Franciscan who had been chaplain and confessor to Queen Catherine of Aragon, was condemned to be burnt. He was suspended in chains from a gallows and among the wood forming the pyre which slowly burnt him to death was the image of Derfel Gadarn, and so in a most curious way the old prophecy that one day the image would set a forest alight was fulfilled.

The image was destroyed, but the wooden horse *ceffyl Derfel*, Dervel's horse, and his *ffon*, his stick or crozier, were still carefully preserved and continued to be venerated. 'The common people used to resort from all parts at Easter in order to have a ride on Derfel's horse. The horse was fixed on a pole, which was placed in a horizontal position, and attached to another, which stood perpendicularly and rested on a pivot. The rider, taking hold of the crozier, which was fastened to the horse, was wheeled round and round, as children are wheeled when they mount a wooden horse at a fair.' A letter written in 1626 to the Bishop of St Asaph by the Rector and Churchwardens of Llandderfel, which refers to 'a wooden image of a Redd Stagg as a relique of the image of Dervell Gadarn' still exists. The fact that the animal had been coloured a dull red — traces of the paint can still be seen — and that its legs are tucked under it, led to it being called a 'stagg'.

The probable reasons why the image of Derfel Gadarn, a little-known Celtic saint, was so highly venerated go far back into history. 'Gadarn' means mighty, and it is thought that there was a link in people's minds between Derfel Gadarn the saint and Hu Gadarn, a mythical hero who with his *dau ychen banwy,* two long-horned oxen, is credited with having dragged a terrible monster out of a lake and so prevented a disastrous flood. Indeed, by some ancient Welsh writers Hu Gadarn's name was linked with Noah, and the tales of his exploits must go back to pre-Christian times. All certain knowledge has been obscured by time, but to this very day the wooden horse and staff can be seen in the porch of Llandderfel Church, an astonishing link with vanished centuries.

It is only a few miles from Llandderfel and the wooden horse to the old church of Llangar which is forever linked with a stag, its present name being a contraction of Llan-garw-gwyn, the church of the white stag. According to legend it was intended to build the church near where Cynwyd bridge spans the river Dee, but as fast as building was done by day, it was pulled down by night. At length the builders were told, supernaturally, to site the church where a white stag should be started. A visiting clergyman, writing to the Bishop of St Asaph in 1729, says: 'The stag was started in a thicket where the church now stands and the boundaries of the Parish on all sides was settled for 'em by this poor deer, where he was forced to run for his life, there lye their bounds, and the rector ought to rejoice that the deer held out so long and took so wide a compass. He fell at last and where he was kill'd is to this day called Moel-y-lladdfa, "The Hill of Slaughter".' The antiquity of Llangar as a place of worship is attested by this legend, for where there are stories about the difficulty of building a church and of supernatural intervention, it is almost certain that there was a struggle for possession of the site between Christian and pagan forces in early days, and quite possibly, yet further back, between rival pagan cults.

Some of the magic of its origin still seems to linger round this little Early English church. It has entirely escaped alteration; in 1860 a new church was built, so the years have slipped away leaving the old edifice with its low but strong walls, its tiny belfry and little dormer windows, virtually unchanged for centuries. Although over 200 years ago it was described as 'standing on a considerable eminence and may securely laugh at the surgings and swellings of the angry Dee, it being strictly and properly built upon a rock', it is not easy to find. It cannot be seen from the road, there is no village near it, and the only means of access is through a gate and across a field. The stone lychgate with the slates of the roof cut to form a pattern is very striking and some of the gravestones have most unusual rests for people to kneel on while praying for the dead. One is always aware of a feeling of sadness when entering a deserted house which once was filled with the business of living; to enter a deserted church, hallowed for centuries by prayer but now abandoned to the elements is even sadder.

As one forces open the heavy oak door and steps into Llangar church the past comes flooding back with a force that is almost tangible. The little building which only measures 20 by 5yd is surprisingly light, owing to the absence of any stained glass. A very fine three-tiered pulpit of carved oak dominates the church; the seating consists mainly of rough benches but there are also some carved pews. The round font is built into the south wall near the door; carved on the huge oak cover which is several inches thick is the date 1711. In the old days the water used for christenings was always brought from a nearby holy well, for it was thought that otherwise the baptized would have ill-luck. The most unusual kneelers made of straw interwoven with strands of blackberry brambles are very solid and surprisingly comfortable to kneel on. Curved oak rails with a little latched gate in the centre guard the small altar, while at the west end of the church a stone staircase leads to quite a spacious gallery which contains benches and a large wooden stand, probably once used for music. On either side of the porch are stone ledges where in former times pedlars used to display and sell their wares.

Another church which owes its origin to an animal can be found in Northern Montgomeryshire. Bounded by the mighty Berwyns to the north, this is one of the wildest and least inhabited parts of Wales; a land of barren crags and desolate moorlands, rivers and waterfalls and little secret valleys up which strangers seldom penetrate. It is therefore not surprising that at the top of one such valley, so narrow that there is only just room for a river and a little land to wind between the mountains, towering up on either side, there is an ancient church with a history as strange and wild as its surroundings, and a story, connected with a hare and stretching back over a thousand years, in which fact and fiction are most curiously woven. The church is called Pennant Melangell, St Melangell's church at the top of the stream.

According to tradition, in Ireland about the seventh century there lived a king with a most beautiful daughter called Melangell. The princess had vowed herself to celibacy, so rather than be forced into marriage by her father she fled from his kingdom, and after many wanderings found refuge near the source of the river Tanat, in this lonely Montgomeryshire valley, where she lived in perfect peace and seclusion for some fifteen years without ever seeing a man. She scorned all material comforts and slept in a crevice in the rocky mountainside, some way above the present road. One day, Brochwell Yscythog, Prince of Powis, was out hunting, and his hounds started up a hare and pursued it into a dense thicket. Bursting through it, the prince was amazed to find in a clearing a most beautiful girl on her knees, deep in prayer, the hare sitting on the folds of her garment, facing the hounds unafraid. The huntsman urged the hounds on, but they fled in terror, howling, and when he tried to blow his horn, it stuck to his lips and no sound came.

When Brochwell heard Melangell's story he was so impressed that he gave her a substantial grant of land at Pennant so that she could found a convent and continue to live unmolested. The privilege of sanctuary was also bestowed with the lands and a curse laid on anyone who violated these rights. St Melangell is said to have lived there as abbess until her death thirty-seven years later and to have performed many miracles 'for those who sought refuge in her sanctuary with pure hearts'. Because hares were under her special protection, for hundreds of years they were known as 'St Melangell's lambs', and even up to the eighteenth century no one in the parish would kill a hare; and if one was chased by a dog and someone called out 'God and St Melangell be with thee' its escape was assured. Often, the strangest legend conceals some fact, and apart from the supernatural element there is no reason to reject the story of a resolute woman defying the hunters. It is also believed that in this remote valley there definitely was a religious community of some kind, as far back as the eighth century, and that by the twelfth century there was a church and shrine dedicated to St Melangell.

It was a day of rain and fitful, September sunshine when I went up the winding hazel-fringed lane to the old church. A deep feeling of peace brooded over the whole valley; no sound, no living thing, disturbed the immemorial silence. The stone lychgate with its gabled roof is dated 1632; the small green in front was used at one time for the performance of miracle plays, and centuries later for cock-fighting. Little now remains of the original church, but the font is twelfth century, and so is a portion of the masonry at the east end of the nave. There is also some late medieval work. The church has been extensively restored on several occasions since the Reformation; the west end of the nave was rebuilt and a tower added early in the seventeenth century; 200 years later the south wall and the tower were rebuilt, additional windows added and existing ones enlarged.

At the back of the church is the fifteenth-century rood screen which now stands 10 ft east of its original position; the elaborate carving on it tells the story of St Melangell. The man on horseback is clearly the Prince of Powis; the huntsman, his horn frozen to his lips, is kneeling nearby. The saint herself is sitting in state in a long robe, her hair flowing, in her left hand a staff, and a large hare chased by two hounds is running towards her. In the eighteenth century Pennant mentions two stone effigies in the churchyard where they suffered very badly from exposure and neglect, but now they lie in safety in the church near the great rood screen. The lady is Melangell; she wears a square headdress and a long pleated gown. Odd little animal faces can just be seen, peering round her waist; rather like pigs, they are probably meant to be hares. The effigy dates from the late fourteenth century, and beside the saint lies the much weatherbeaten figure of a man in armour, Madog ap Iorweth, his sword partly drawn, his head uncovered, which is rare. Propped up against the effigies is an enormous curved bone, like a great elephant's tusk — it was found on the Berwyn mountains and is called the Giant's Rib.

The unique feature of this lonely church is the small room built on at the east end. It is called *cell-y-bedd*, the cell of the grave, and here it seems certain that St Melangell was buried and later her relics kept; often in bygone centuries, the relics of a saint, or perhaps the whole body, were housed in a shrine in a church instead of being interred, so that they could be more easily venerated. Travellers in the eighteenth and nineteenth centuries say that the little room was used as a vestry but they saw fragments of the old shrine; indeed until quite recently a number of stones, beautifully sculptured and ornamented, were built into the lychgate and the fabric of the church. Then in 1958 experts excavated the *cell-y-bedd*. Under the wooden floor, stones and rubble were discovered, and lower still a cobbled floor into which was set a stone slab measuring 2ft 6in by 5ft 8in. Digging beneath this stone enough evidence was found, including fragments of human bones which were later reinterred, to establish that this was indeed the remains of a very early Christian burial place.

It was customary for the stone chest which contained the relics to be raised on a structure of arches and columns, and above the chest there would be a gabled roof. Enough stones from what was the shrine of St Melangell have been recovered to convince experts that the shrine was certainly twelfth-century work, possibly as early as 1160-70. Now the whole shrine has been meticulously restored, the most important stones have been rebuilt into the new shrine and once again the lovely capitals, demi-columns and elaborately carved gables can be seen in their rightful setting.

The little building that houses the shrine has also been rebuilt and a tablet in the north wall states that the Montgomeryshire County Council restored the shrine with £200 from the Welsh Church Acts Fund, 1958. It is a place of beauty and extraordinary peace, and even after the lapse of so many centuries still seems pervaded with the powerful spirit of the indomitable young woman who fled from the comforts of her father's court in Ireland and by the sheer force of her personality was able to wrest a considerable amount of land, together with special privileges, from a wild and ruthless Welsh chieftain. When I last visited the shrine a vase of fresh flowers on the floor of *cell-y-bedd* showed that she is still remembered by the people of her valley.

Through St Tydecho, its founder, Mallwyd church some twelve miles from Dolgellau is also connected with animals, for the saint was well-known for his power over wild beasts. According to tradition he lived in the fifth or sixth century and was an abbot in Armorica till he came to spread the Gospel in this remote part of Wales, where he lived the life of a hermit, wearing a hair shirt, sleeping on stones and cultivating land sufficient for his spartan needs. But though he lived such a simple life he incurred the wrath of Maelgwyn Gwynedd, a local chieftain, who to make things difficult for the saint sent him a stud of valuable white horses to look after. Tydecho turned them loose among the mountains where they ran wild and ungroomed. When Maelgwyn wanted them returned they were in such poor condition he was very angry with the saint and as a reprisal seized Tydecho's oxen, so that he could not plough and harrow his land.

The saint must have been in despair, but some stags appeared and allowed themselves to be yoked to the plough, while out of a nearby forest came a wolf, so tame he could be used to draw the harrow. However, things continued to be so unpleasant for St Tydecho in North Wales that finally he returned to Brittany, not before he had founded two churches, one of them at Mallwyd, the other at Llanymawddwy.

Many ancient and beautiful little places of worship in Wales have been so ruthlessly altered by the heavy hand of Victorian restorers that they have lost much of their interest, but fortunately this has not been the fate of Mallwyd. St Tydecho's sanctuary, part of which dates from the fourteenth century, is of great interest both archaeologically and historically. It consists of a simple parallelogram with no division between the nave and the chancel. The roof of the latter is coved; the nave is waggon-roofed and plastered between the beams. The west end is very unusual, for benches rise in rows nearly up to the roof on either side of a door leading into the lower part of the belfry which is used as a vestry.

The tower is probably unique. The lower part to just above the roof of the nave is stone and this is capped by a square timber belfry, supported not by the walls of the tower but by four massive oak posts, some 12in square, carried down to ground level. On the south side of the belfry, near the top, the words 'Soli Deo sac(rum) Anno Christi MDCXL' made by perforations through the boards can just be seen, and two dormer windows near the belfry add to the quaint appearance of the church. The bells date from 1642. On a massive oak beam across the porch is inscribed C. 1641.H., and above are two enormous bones, said to be the skull and rib of a prehistoric animal which, according to local tradition, were dug up in Cae Llan, a field on the banks of the nearby river Dovey that flows a short distance from the church. A contributor to the *Archaeologia Cambrensis* in 1901 said the bones had been over the porch for at least a hundred years.

During medieval times the parishioners of Mallwyd owned herds of cattle which they grazed on pastures and on the lower slopes of the mountains, the profits being used to pay priests for special purposes, as was done in some other Merioneth parishes. A note written at the end of the reign of Henry VIII states that there is 'due to this priest [the incumbent of Mallwyd] for parcel of his wages at Mayday last which he should have received of this year's increase of cattle, 26s 8d.'

Of the priests who from 1290 onwards served Mallwyd, by far the most distinguished was Dr John Davies, one of the greatest of Welsh scholars, Rector from 1604 to 1644. The 1620 edition of the Welsh Bible is known as Richard Parry's Bible but nowadays it is considered that much of the credit for the uniformity and correctness of the language was due to John Davies of Mallwyd and that he also probably had a good deal to do with the 1621 edition of the Welsh *Book of Common Prayer*. His best-known work was published in 1621 under the title *Antiquae Linguae Britannicae . . . Rudimenta*. It was one of the earliest grammars in the Welsh language; this was followed in 1632 by the *Dictionarium Duplex*, a Welsh-Latin Dictionary in two parts.

But in spite of all his literary activities — when his dictionary was being published he spent a whole year in London — he worked hard for his parishioners. He restored and enlarged the church and built three bridges, one of them in 1635. He was a man of forceful character and stalwartly refused to give way on matters of principle. When Archbishop

Laud ordered that in all churches the altar should stand at the east end, not in the middle of the chancel, Dr Davies refused to obey, and until probably the beginning of the nineteenth century the altar remained in the centre of the chancel, opposite the reading desk. The present altar was given in 1732 by R. Mytton of Shropshire and is made of blue-black marble.

Dr Davies died in 1644 and was buried in the chancel of his church. The Latin inscription that marked his grave became almost indecipherable, though a copy has been preserved in the Diocesan Archives, and an appeal was launched so that a new tablet could be installed. This was done in 1970, a particularly appropriate year, marking the 350th anniversary of the revised translation of the Bible into Welsh with which Dr Davies was so deeply involved.

At the Communion Service at Mallwyd a curious old custom is still observed, the women taking Communion first, then the men. At Llanymawddwy, St Tyecho's other church, this custom is also observed, but here the sexes are strictly segregated, the women sitting on one side of the church, the men on the other.

Lord Newborough's privately owned little Anglican chapel is of special interest because of its marvellous examples of Welsh craftsmanship. The chapel stands in a secluded corner of his estate at Rug — pronounced Reeg — in the parish of Corwen, and is known as 'the Chapel of the Trinity in Edeirnion'. Though quite near a busy main road it is so shrouded by trees that few passers-by notice it.

A simple rectangular building of grey stone, it measures about 40 by 25ft, with a door and a small belfry at the west end. It is not known where it originally stood, but Colonel William Salesbury of Rug (1580-1660), an ancestor of Lord Newborough, had it moved to the present site in 1637. The Colonel, or *Hen Hosanau Gleisien*, Old Blue Stockings as he was called because he wore hose of that colour, was a rich, colourful character; a great lover of literature he wrote a good deal of religious verse in Welsh. He had led an adventurous life but it is for his gallant and lengthy defence of Denbigh Castle — the last fortress in Wales to hold out for Charles I — that he is best known. According to family tradition, so great was Cromwell's admiration for the Colonel's courage and loyalty that he gave General Ironside orders that Rug chapel was not to be damaged in any way.

A Deed of Endowment, 3 January 1641, provided an annual income of £12 for a curate or chaplain, and stipulated that the service should be taken by 'one discrete and completely learned scholar of good character and behaviour; being a sensible reader and minister within Holy Orders'. He had to be Welsh-speaking so he could take 'Divine Service and other Holy Exercises in the native and vulgarly known tongue' twice each Sunday. During the eighteenth century, the then owner of Rug, Sir Robert Williames Vaughan, augmented the stipend by £2,000 invested in Consols.

It is said that Colonel Salesbury had the chapel built to save himself the irritation of listening to the Rector of nearby Corwen, whom he described as a Michaiah, son of Imlah, 'who doth not prophesy good concerning me but only evil'. The chapel is in the diocese of St Asaph and seems to have been a source of annoyance to succeeding bishops, possibly because it was privately owned so they had no jurisdiction over it. Indeed, so bitter were the feelings against the lovely little place of worship that it has been called *capel-y-genfigen*, the chapel of envy.

The exterior is so austere that when one sees the spectacular interior, the magnificent wooden roof, the elaborate carvings and the glowing colours of the paintings on the roof and walls, the reds, golds, greens, greys and blues, only slightly muted by time, one experiences a sense almost of shock, passing as it were instantaneously from the twentieth to the seventeenth century. The architect and archaeologist Douglas Hague described the roof as consisting 'of five collar beam trusses

ANIMALS AND SAINTS IN WELSH FOLKLORE

with moulded soffets and two cusped struts . . . The central truss and those against the East and West walls are of a quasi hammer-beam type, their ends being carried on short brackets sprung from wall posts.' These brackets may be medieval and carry carved wooden angels, still very lovely, though despite Cromwell's orders the candles they held were removed. Floral designs, most beautifully painted in rich colours, decorate all the trusses. On one is the date 1637, divided by the letters IHS. On each side of the date are painted sunflowers, symbolising faithfulness. Much of the roof and also the very elaborately panelled frieze of carved wood between the lowest purlins and the top of the walls are beautifully carved and painted with animals and strange monsters, such as a two-headed lamb, a dragon and a crouching horse with a serpent round its body.

On the north wall of the nave is a very strange painted memorial. The inscriptions above and below the skeleton are in Welsh and could be translated 'As the light of the candle exhausts the tallow, so the fires of life die,' and 'Life however long it may be, dies day by day and night by night.' Unusual features are the canopied pews, reserved for the family, on either side of the altar. On one of them two heads are carved, said to represent King Charles and Colonel Salesbury. A very beautiful angel is painted on the middle panel of the altar which is in the form of a chest; rather curiously, the top is designed to slide off.

The benches in the nave, which originally had no backs, are placed across longitudinals along which are carved extraordinary animals, more usual in an Elizabethan bestiary than a Christian church. They include dragons, a cow's face with a serpent on either side, a pelican with her young and a donkey. The White Ensign hanging from the comparatively modern chancel screen was carried on the yacht commanded by the present Lord Newborough during the evacuation of the British Expeditionary Force from Dunkirk in 1940.

Hanging from the central truss of the roof is a curious wooden candelabrum. Except for the box at the base and a few plain struts, it was made on a lathe. Electricity has replaced candles, otherwise the candelabrum has remained unchanged through the centuries. The chapel was never consecrated so when relations of Lord Newborough wished to be married there, a special licence had to be obtained from the Archbishop of Canterbury.

Near the west door is a medieval cross shaft placed there after the death of Colonel Salesbury. Originally it stood near the castle he so bravely defended and it is surmounted by a cross of a much later date that came from the gable end of the chapel. The land surrounding the chapel is full of trees, shrubs and huge rhododendrons that through the years have run riot, in one place meeting overhead to form a tunnel across the path leading to the only consecrated piece of land. Here, three members of Lord Newborough's family are buried, in a very peaceful place shaded by massive Wellingtonias.

Nonconformity plays such a large part in the religious life of Wales that mention must be made of the little chapels to be found in so many parts. Though they can in no way compare with the great Anglican cathedrals and churches, yet the very simplicity of their architecture gives them a charm all their own, and the stories which lie behind the building of so many of them throw interesting light on an aspect of the social conditions and customs of the past which perhaps is not widely known. Nowadays when great efforts are being made to bring together the many branches of the Christian faith, the unbridgeable gulf of bigotry and hatred which once divided church from chapel seems incredible, but that it did exist is proved only too conclusively by the early history of nonconformity in the isolated parish of Llanfachreth, Merioneth, which is typical of a number of other places in Wales. Even in my childhood traces of this intolerance remained; some farmers were afraid to be caught going to chapel in case they could not get their cottages and barns repaired by the squire, who even looked with great disfavour on my father because he employed a nonconformist maid at the vicarage.

The first Methodist service to be held in Llanfachreth Parish was in 1783, beside a lonely lake. The service had to be out of doors for no one dared ask a minister to their house: the local landowners were staunch Anglicans and violently opposed to Dissent. Edward Corbett of Ynys-y-maengwyn, a kindly, tolerant man in all other respects, even set his foxhounds on some Methodists, and Sir Robert Williames Vaughan of Nannau, 1788-1843, an equally enlightened landowner, would allow no chapel to be built on his extensive estates. After fifteen years of desperate effort the Methodists found a site for their chapel in the village of Llanfachreth. But even then their troubles were not at an end. The only available building material in those days were stones and none could be found to build the chapel, for although there were plenty everywhere, Sir Robert not only refused to sell any, but also persuaded another landowner, who had been favourably inclined towards nonconformity, to follow his example. Fortunately, however, the site was so rocky that when the foundations were dug, enough stone was excavated, which together with the stones from a derelict house belonging to the Methodists provided enough material to build Capel Bethel. It was opened in 1801; benches were provided for the worshippers and the earthen floor was strewn in winter with rushes in an attempt to keep people's feet warm. Enlarged in 1848, the chapel as it is today was completed in 1868. As is quite usual in Wales, a house was built on to the chapel where a caretaker could live.

By 1838 the Independents had so increased in numbers that they required a chapel of their own, but like the Methodists they found it very difficult to find a site and building stones. At last a friendly landowner offered stones to the Independents, but unfortunately they were situated several miles away from the building site, and had to be carried by horse and cart. One can imagine the immense amount of gruelling work entailed in loading and unloading the great stones and transporting them, in addition to a hard day's work. The chapel was completed in 1879. Its simplicity and pleasing proportions give it almost a Georgian look, and situated in a remote place, near a turbulent mountain torrent, it is rather charmingly called Capel Ffrwd-yr-hebog, the chapel of the hawks' stream, and indeed raptors often hover over the quiet burial ground which in summer is bright with devil's-bit scabious and heather.

Another isolated chapel, Carmel, stands on the lower slopes of Rhobell, a rocky, forbidding mountain, stretching up for nearly 3,000 feet. This lonely place was chosen — even today the only road to it is very narrow and precipitous — because it was the only site available. It cost £160 to build in 1874. A couple lived in the chapel house, rent and rates free, were paid 8s a year and in return performed certain duties which included providing food for the visiting minister — at not more than 6d a meal — and looking after his horse.

Sunday Schools formed a very important part of the nonconformists' religious life. The devotion of the teachers must have been great, for to reach their classes many of them had to walk long distances along rough, steep roads or over mountain tracks, on their one day of rest after a week's hard manual labour. Some were very colourful characters, like Cadwaladr Lewis, 1755-1832, who though a devout Methodist could tell the most extraordinary stories of the supernatural. He even claimed that one night he had raised the devil and only escaped from his clutches when at dawn a nearby cock crowed.

The northern part of the Llanfachreth parish was a land of barren mountains, desolate moorlands and few farms. Before becoming nonconformists, the inhabitants were as wild as their environment, immorality was rife, cock-fighting a favourite pastime and many of the men drank heavily. Sundays were mostly devoted to various games, including football, and sometimes fairs, when mostly horses, but also dogs and cats, were auctioned. A number of people attended the fairs and in the evening came drinking, wrestling and fierce fighting. The swearing was so loud that it was said it could be heard seven miles away!

In the 1780s the Nonconformists made a serious effort to convert these tough people. No one dared offer hospitality because of the squire's hatred of dissenters, so the first service in the district was to be in the open air, and filled with curiosity a number of people came to witness so unusual an event. It must have been a very pleasant scene, for while they waited the women knitted and the men fished in the River Mawddach, which being near its source was just a small stream, flowing peacefully through level fields. But the crowd was a brutal one and when the preacher and his friends arrived, they were set on so fiercely that they had to run for their lives. One man was unlucky, for he was caught by Ned, the servant from a nearby farm, who was so powerful he could fell an ox with his stick. He was thrashing his victim so unmercifully with a heavy whip that only the intervention of a couple of men prevented his murder.

Little by little the Nonconformists gained so many converts in the district that two chapels were built in the nineteenth century; one, Abergeirw, a stone's throw from where the preacher was nearly murdered, and the other, Hermon, in a rather eerie place, surrounded by trees. Anglicans long regarded Nonconformity with suspicion and the meeting places had by law to be reported to the diocesan bishop by the parish priest. This was still done as late as 1825.

Sad to say, the future of these little chapels, like many others in Wales — the visible symbol of such fervent faith and such heroic effort — is bleak indeed. Congregations and support are dwindling.

No one can say with certainty when or with whom the Gospel first came to Wales, but it is certain that after the Roman Legions had marched away forever and hordes of invaders came pillaging and destroying from the East, Christianity did re-enter Wales, this time from Gaul and Brittany along the Western sea routes; indeed, with the disintegration of the *Pax Romana*, the ancient seaways became the chief link between Wales and what remained of civilisation on the continent. Numbers of missionaries crossed the treacherous waters to the coastal areas of Wales and gradually penetrated inland, so that by the time St Augustine reached Kent in 597 there had been a flourishing Celtic Church in Wales for a considerable time. During the fifth and sixth centuries there was such an upsurge of Christianity, such a rekindling of faith, that this period was called 'The Age of Saints', and Wales might almost have been called the Land of Saints — on Bardsey Island 20,000 were said to be buried, for to the Celtic mind a saint was merely a man who had entered the religious profession and he was then called by that title whatever his mode of life. Of the 500 Welsh saints whose names are known, only St David was actually canonised. In its original form canonisation meant that the person's name was included in the Canon of the Mass, a privilege granted only by the Pope.

Many of the Welsh saints are now forgotten, but a few have become legendary figures, whose personalities seem to blaze across the darkness of the centuries; in their lives fact and fiction are so interwoven that they can scarcely be disentangled, the one almost as strange as the other. Such a man was St Beuno, whose great cruciform church at Clynnog Fawr on the Lleyn Peninsula, overshadowed by mountains and within sight of the sea, is one of the ecclesiastical wonders of North Wales; it has been called the 'fairest church in all Caernarvonshire'. The story of its foundation is even stranger than its presence in so isolated a place.

St Beuno came from Powys to North Wales about the year 616 and was given land by King Cadwallon on which to build a church. In return the saint presented his benefactor with a golden sceptre worth sixty cows. While foundations for the church were being dug a woman came along with a baby which would not stop crying. When St Beuno told the woman to quieten it she said, 'How can I, when you are taking land that should belong to this child?' This injustice upset St Beuno very much and he immediately went to King Cadwallon and told him the land must be restored to its rightful owner and that he himself must be given some other land or he would demand the return of the golden sceptre. The King contemptuously refused; St Beuno cursed him — Celtic saints had the power to do this — and left his court in a rage. Soon after the King's cousin found the infuriated saint sitting on a large stone, and 'for his own soul's sake and that of Cadwallon's' gave St Beuno some of his own land at Clynnog Fawr. The stone over which the transaction was ratified is in Clynnog Fawr Church; it is called *Maen Beuno*, Beuno's Stone. It is 4ft high with an incised cross on it which the saint is said to have traced with two strokes of his thumb.

Nothing remains of the original church, built some thirteen hundred years ago, nor of the community or *clas* which he founded. These *clasau* were centres of teaching and learning and also bases from which priests could go out into the surrounding districts, make new converts and found more churches or 'cells' which, at first at any rate, were under the jurisdiction of the *clas*. Those who lived in them were termed *claswr* or canons, never monks, and at their head was an abbot. The original church of Clynnog was probably destroyed in a Danish raid in 978, but another must soon have been built as there are references to it in the tenth and twelfth centuries which stress its great importance. By 1291 it was a portionary church with five prebends, and later it became collegiate.

153

Most of the present church dates from the beginning of the sixteenth century. When Leland visited it between 1536 and 1539 he noted 'The church that is now there with cross aisles is about as big as Saint David's, but is of new work ... better than Bangor'. It is indeed a magnificent structure, with nave, chancel, north and south transepts, and a square tower at the west end which was probably built after Leland's visit. The fine screen in front of the chancel has been skilfully restored; the prebends' seats are well preserved, and the fine panelling of the nave should not be missed. One is struck by the feeling of spaciousness, and because there is no stained glass and the windows are large — almost the entire east wall consists of glass — on a bright spring morning the whole place seems drenched with light, and the chattering of the jackdaws outside emphasises rather than disturbs the immemorial peace within.

At the south-west side of the church is a narrow passage about 5yd long which at one time was used as a lock-up. It leads to a chapel, measuring 42 by 24ft, called *eglwys-bedd*, the Shrine of St Beuno, for it is here he is said to have been buried. According to legend when he died and his corpse was brought to Clynnog Fawr for burial, a violent quarrel broke out because the communities at Bardsey Island and Nevin also wanted the saint's remains. The disputants agreed to wait until morning. Miraculously, when day dawned there were found to be three identical coffins, so everyone was satisfied and there were three burials, but Clynnog people maintained that they actually had St Beuno's body. When the chapel was restored in 1913, beneath and near it the foundations of a very much earlier building were found, which may well have belonged to the original chapel.

As in life, so in death, St Beuno was a powerful worker of miracles. For hundreds of years his plain altar tomb was covered with rushes on which sick people were laid after bathing in his well about a quarter of a mile from the church;

they fervently believed that if they spent the night there they would be cured. Pennant, writing in 1770, says, 'I myself once saw on the tomb a feather bed on which a poor paralytic from Merioneddshire had lain the whole night.' The tomb was still standing in 1790 but all traces of it have since vanished and as late as 1850 the chapel was used as a school 'in which about fifty children are gratuitously instructed by subscription'. Many miraculous stories are told of St Beuno. It was said he could walk on the sea and one evening when he was returning from Anglesey in this unusual way, he was much disturbed to find he had lost his precious book of sermons. But when he reached the beach just below Clynnog, there was the book on a stone, guarded by a curlew. In gratitude the saint blessed the birds and from henceforth curlews' nests were difficult to find.

The Welsh princes richly endowed the church and the many pilgrims passing through Clynnog from North Wales to the sacred island of Bardsey provided valuable revenue; so did the gifts put into *'Cyff Beuno'* — St Beuno's Chest — which can still be seen in the church. This chest, including the lid, hollowed out of a single piece of an ash tree, bound with iron and with three great locks, is 3ft 9in long. Money was dropped through the slit in the lid as a kind of sin offering; a Reverend Evans, writing in 1812, says a manuscript was found in the chest containing the words, 'Here I offer to God four pence for my private sins, on which account the Almighty is now punishing me; to be given for the same service, that the blessed saints used to offer, in the name of the Father, the Son and the Holy Ghost, Amen.' Money from the sale of all lambs and calves in the neighbourhood which had a peculiar slit in their ears, called *nod Beuno* — Beuno's mark — was also put in the chest. Farmers brought animals to the church wardens on Trinity Sunday for sale, and this custom, mentioned by Leland in 1589, continued until the nineteenth century, as did offerings for the well. On Trinity Sunday, also, bread and cheese were offered to the saint, 'and a great piece, if procurable, was almost a certain cure for the worst case, bodily or spiritual'. After thirteen hundred years St Beuno is still remembered, for he was so revered and loved that there are more churches dedicated to him in North Wales than to any other saint.

The Cistercian monks were greatly loved in Wales where they founded a number of magnificent abbeys, sited in lonely and beautiful places. Cymer Abbey was built some two miles west of Dolgellau where the river Mawddach broadens out into an estuary of unsurpassed beauty and is joined by the river Wnion. Hence the name Cymer—pronounced Kummer — which means a 'confluence'.

The abbey, one of the last to be built, originally consisted of a large church, a side chapel, cloisters, a chapter house and various other buildings; but now only the ruins of the church stand. It was under the patronage of Maredudd ap Cynan, Lord of Merioneth, and was founded in 1198 or 1199 by monks from Abbey Cym Hir in Radnorshire. An old writer remarks that 'It seems that it was a colony of monks they sent away from Abbey Cwm Hir, as bees do, when the hive is too full'.

The last Llewelyn had a special fondness for Cymer Abbey: he granted it a most generous Charter, and in 1283 as he marched southwards from Snowdonia to fight the invading English, he left a small package at the abbey for safe-keeping till his return. But he was killed near Builth, Welsh resistance crumbled, and Roger L'Estrange arrived at Cymer Abbey, demanding Llewelyn's property in the name of the King. Among the jewels left behind are said to have been the Crown of Gwynedd which Welsh princes had worn for something like eight hundred years, and a piece of the true cross, richly encrusted with jewels. In his *Genealogical History*, Sandford tells that 'Alphonso, who died at 10 years of age and was the third son of Edward I, offered up the golden coronet of Llewelyn, Prince of Wales and other jewels at the Tomb of St Edward, Westminster, when his Father and Mother returned unto England from Jerusalem'. It is said that the piece of the true cross was kept in the Tower of London until it was destroyed by Cromwell.

The Cistercians were practical Christians who believed in teaching the people useful crafts as well as religion. By better methods of sheep breeding they vastly improved the Welsh wool trade, or the Staple as it was then called. The names of two fields, one on either side of the stone bridge over Mawddach near the abbey, are a reminder of the wool trade: *cae-y-stapl*, the fields of the staple. Ships used to ply round the coasts and come up the estuary to where the bridge now stands to collect the monks' bales of wool. Another field was called *cae-y-llong*, the field of the ship, and here probably the vessels were moored. The Cistercians also taught people about the smelting of iron and lead. The abbey had two forges, and near a farm called *dol-y-clochydd*, the meadow of the bell ringer, where the bell ringer from Cymer used to live, may be seen the remains of an old forge.

The monks of Cymer were also great apiarists, for the valley where the abbey stood has always been famous for the quality of its honey. Only candles made from beeswax could be used when Mass was being celebrated for there was supposed to be a divine blessing upon bees. Wotton's *Leges Wallicia* refers to this: 'Bees derive their noble descent from Paradise: when, owing to man's transgressions they were thence expelled, God gave them His blessing: on this account Mass cannot properly be sung without their wax'.

Hospitality to travellers was another facet of Cymer Abbey's life. The main road between the Lordships of Ardudwy and Bala ran near the abbey and as in those days there was no bridge over the river Mawddach, and to cross it after dark was unsafe, travellers often had to spend the night by its banks. The kindly monks often gave their hospitality to the wayfarers — the landing stage by the river is still called *Marian Rhad,* Strand of Grace, and those long-ago travellers are still called to mind by the names of nearby fields: *Dol-saesonaeg,* the English Meadow, and *Cae-y-meirch,* the Horses' field. Giraldus Cambrensis had great difficulty in getting over the Mawddach and does not seem to have been at all favourably impressed, for he said, 'It is the wildest and roughest district in all Wales.'

Total disaster nearly overtook the abbey during Henry III's reign. Rebellion broke out and the King himself led an army into the Principality. A monk from Cymer was captured and when questioned by the King gave entirely false information, with the result that the English were tricked into crossing very marshy land where they got bogged down and were slaughtered without mercy by the Welsh who had been lying in wait for them. The famous Plantagenet rage knew no bounds. Henry ordered the entire abbey to be razed to the ground, and much of it was destroyed, but by paying the enormous fine of 300 marks the Abbot was able to save the church and some of the monastic buildings.

Though the abbey was a poor one and only of local importance, it possessed two unique treasures, a superb silver-gilt chalice and paten. However shortly before the Dissolution of the Monasteries in 1536 they disappeared and for over 350 years no trace of them could be found. Then one evening in February 1890, Ellis Jones and Griffith Griffiths, who were employed by T. H. Roberts of Dolgellau to prospect for gold among the mountains north of the Barmouth-Dolgellau road near Llanelltyd, were making their way to their homes in Llanfachreth, a tiny village hidden away in the mountains north of Dolgellau. As they trudged along the narrow tracks, winding between heather and great grey boulders over Y Garn mountain — a more desolate place would be hard to imagine — they stumbled upon what they thought was an ordinary metal cup and plate.

Though they were so black with age and coated with soil that they appeared valueless, the men decided to take them home and naturally told their friends about this curious find.

Very soon, to their intense surprise, two men called on them and said they had no right to this strange cup and plate and might get into serious trouble if they kept them, so they had better hand them over. Griffith and Ellis were upset at this, and gave their find to their visitors, who promptly sold them for 50s. Mr Roberts, their employer, heard of the transaction and was able to secure the cup and paten, which was indeed fortunate for it was soon established that they were the long-lost silver-gilt items from Cymer Abbey, two of the most perfect examples of late thirteenth-century church plate in existence.

The chalice is 7¾in high; an inscription at the foot reads *'Nicolys me fecit de Herfordie'*. This Nicolas has never been identified for certain, but he might have been the celebrated divine called 'Nicolas (or Nicholas) Herfordie' who was Chancellor of Hereford Cathedral in 1377 and treasurer in 1398. Only two English medieval chalices are taller; one at Leominster and the other at Trinity College, Oxford. The paten, too, is massively made, 7⁵⁄₁₆in in diameter and probably the largest known English example. The centre is engraved with a seated figure of Christ, his right hand raised in blessing, in his left holding a book upon his knee. Around him are the symbols of the four evangelists and circles which represent the nimbus; all these are surrounded by the inscription: *'In Nomine: Patris: et Filii: et Spiritus Sancti Am(en).'*

News of the almost miraculous discovery soon spread far beyond Dolgellau, and on 14 June 1890 an article about it appeared in *The Illustrated London News* and sparked off a controversy that was to last many years. Promptly the Crown stepped in and in a letter dated 18 June 1890 to Mr Roberts claimed the chalice and paten as treasure trove, and stated that unless they were handed over, legal steps would be taken, because 'It is the duty of a person finding any treasure to report its find to the Crown, failure to do so amounts to a commission of an offence. If the treasure is NOT treasure trove it became the property of the finder unless the true owner can be found.'

But Mr Roberts and his friends, one of whom was Pritchard Morgan, the well-known gold pioneer and at that time Member of Parliament for Merthyr Tydfil, would not give way and the claims of the Crown were not pressed, until the publicity given to the sale in 1892 at Christies of the chalice and paten for £710, and their subsequent resale to Baron Schroder for £3,000, brought the whole affair into the limelight again. Then the Crown started legal action in earnest, seeking to prove that the vessels were 'treasure trove'. This was hard to establish, for treasure is not 'treasure trove' if it is just abandoned or lost; it is only 'where any gold or silver or coin, plate or bullion is found concealed in a house or in the earth or any other private place, the owner thereof being unknown'. The crux of the matter was whether the vessels had been merely abandoned or had they been carefully hidden? This is almost impossible to decide, but probably when it became known that the abbey was to be dissolved someone connected with Cymer spirited the vessels away so they should not fall into the hands of the King's agents. One wonders whether the Abbot knew, for if his connivance could be proved he would have lost the pension granted to dispossessed abbots; yet surely someone in authority must have been involved — no servant would have dared run such a risk? Possibly whoever took the vessels away was pursued by the King's representatives and abandoned the treasures in his haste to escape, but this does not seem likely; they weighed a mere 46oz and when found were close together — not lying as though thrown away in haste.

It seems more likely that they were deliberately hidden, for the place where they were discovered was not far from two farms, Cwm-mynach-ganol and Cwm-mynach-isa, which by their names — *mynach* meaning a monk — must have had some connection with the abbey. If it was decided to hide the chalice and paten, the monks might well have thought of these farms, tucked away among the mountains, inaccessible and remote; then perhaps on second thoughts it was considered even safer to hide them at a little distance from the farms. One wonders why they were never recovered by those who hid them, but there must have been a tremendous hue and cry when the King's agents found that the only treasure of the little abbey had disappeared, and some years would have had to elapse before it was safe to retrieve them. Perhaps by then those who had hidden them had died or could not, amid that desolate waste of heather and rocks, find the hiding place — approximately half a mile in a straight line to the east of Cwm-mynach-isa farm in the parish of Llanaber, and approximately two miles from the junction of the Barmouth-Penmaenpool road.

Before proceedings had gone very far, Baron Schroder let it be known that if he might keep the vessels for his lifetime he would bequeath them to the monarch, an offer which the Crown accepted — no doubt with relief — and litigation ceased. Baron Schroder died on 20 May 1910, and in his will was the following clause:

> I bequeath the chalice and paten, or wafer dish, which was discovered near Dolgelley in the County of Merioneth, in Wales, and which was some years since purchased by me, to His Majesty the King, his heirs and successors, to be disposed of for the public service in such manner as His Majesty, his heirs and successors, or the Lords Commissioners of the Treasury for the time being on his or their behalf, shall direct.

Even then the controversy was not quite at an end, for where were the chalice and paten to go? In the end, these relics of the past which though actually discovered within the boundaries of Llanaber Parish are always known as the Dolgellau chalice and paten, quite rightly found a secure haven in the National Museum of Wales, Cardiff; in deference, I have always heard, to the personal wishes of King George V. But what of the men who found the priceless treasure? I knew Griffith Griffiths and Ellis Jones when I was a child and it is sad that they never received any reward or recognition.

After the monks left Cymer, the site remained in the possession of the Crown till Queen Elizabeth I gave it to Robert, Earl of Leicester. In the course of time, it passed to the Vaughans of Nannau, where it remained until 1930, when the late General John Vaughan placed the buildings under the guardianship of the Ministry of Works. The gentle monks have gone forever, leaving few traces behind them. Their abbey is in ruins and their ancient burial place on the hillside is now a field where sheep and cattle graze. But every springtime, according to tradition, this particular spot, unlike any of the other nearby fields, is white with flowers, a tribute, maybe, to the White Fathers and their abbey, still one of the treasures of Merioneth.

It must be wondered why the names of so many churches in Wales begin with *Llan*. This prefix originally meant an enclosure and is found in such secular words as *gwinllan*, a vineyard, and *corlan*, a fold. A.W. Wade-Evans, in *Welsh Christian Origins*, says, 'In Wales the more general name for a monastery was "Llan". At first it denoted land appropriated for a definite purpose, as for example the site of a monastery. Then it designated the building on the land ... In the process of time "llan" became more of a church than a monastery, it bore its later meaning of simply "church". The number of "llans" in Wales, says Newell, is about 510.'

162

On a little eminence near Cymer Abbey stands an ancient 'Llan' which is dedicated to Illtyd, one of the greatest of the Celtic saints, who flourished during the fifth and sixth centuries. After so many centuries it is difficult to be certain about St Illtyd's origins. Some say he was born in Wales, others that he first came to these shores from Brittany as a soldier to help King Arthur fight his pagan foes. But it is certain he was a cultured and learned man; he was head of the famous college at Llantwit Major, Glamorganshire, founded about the year 500, which was an immense spiritual storehouse and a great seat of learning, from whence men went out to spread the Gospel all over the Western world.

In the course of time St Illtyd, some thirteen hundred years ago, came to the banks of the river Mawddach and built a church. It was customary in those days to found places of worship, also used partly as retreats, on land given by the chief of the tribe to whom the missionary came. Contrary to present-day ideas, places far removed from human habitation were chosen and it was only with the passing of the centuries that settlements like Llanelltyd village grew around the church.

Nothing is known of the earliest building but it would probably have been a rude structure of daub and wattle. The *Taxatio* of 1291 specifically mentions a church at Llanelltyd, and it is known that the monks of the nearby Cistercian Abbey at Cymer served it until the Dissolution of the Monasteries in 1536. At a date unknown a stone church was built; it was altered several times, but the walls of the present building are for the most part old, some dating from the Perpendicular period. Of special interest are the very unusual upper windows on the south side, which may well be early Tudor; unfortunately similar ones on the north wall have long since been done away with. At the west end is a pointed stone bell-cot for one bell, carried on stone corbels which seem to be ancient.

Entering the church, a small single-chamber structure,

through a great oak door on the north side, dated 1779, one is immediately struck by the marvellous wooden beams of the fifth-century roof. The unusual panelling round the walls was made from the pews used by the congregation before the church was extensively restored in 1899, and interesting features are the four lancet panels with corona on either side of the altar. The ones on the north side are fifteenth century; the matching ones on the south side are modern.

The inscribed stone at the west end is noteworthy, being believed to be the only one of its kind in the British Isles. On the top is an incised footprint and underneath an inscription which has been interpreted as 'The mark of Rhoderic [or Rhyddllech] is on this stone which he placed there when he set out on a pilgrimage.' Nothing is known of the pilgrim or where he went, but it used to be thought that incising a footprint on a stone ensured a safe return and at one time many Welsh sailors held this superstition. This particular relic was found in 1876 near the church under a pile of rubbish in an old outhouse.

Though there have been two additions to the graveyard in modern times, Llanelltyd Church still stands in the centre of a circular burial ground, one of the best examples in existence and probably well over a thousand years old. Circular burial grounds are of great antiquity; rectangular-shaped ones were introduced much later from the continent and the custom was continued by the church in Norman and medieval times. The old Celtic preference for a circular or sub-circular burial place may have been Druidic in origin and it has been suggested that Llanelltyd Church was built on the site of a stone circle. The tenth-century Laws of Hywel Dda state that 'the measure of a burial ground is a legal erw [an acre] in length with its end to the churchyard; and that circling the churchyard is to be its compass.'

This is how it is thought the limits of the circular churchyard were fixed. Before the church was built, a man stood where the altar would be, and in his outstretched hand held a rod, its length based on the measurements of the yoke of his plough team. With outstretched arm he circled the site of the altar, and all the land within the circle which was called an *erw* became sacred. Within, God extended His protection not only to the dead, but also to the living, however heinous their crime might be. Hence the expression 'God's Acre' for a churchyard, and the old custom that a wanted man could claim sanctuary within a churchyard for up to seven years and seven days.

Near Llanelltyd church is an old house, recently modernised but still called Tyn 'y llan, the Church House, or Yr Hen Dafarn, the Old Tavern. Until comparatively recent times, people often had to walk or ride many miles to attend services, and at the end of their journey they were in need of rest and refreshment. The church authorities wisely realised that it was impossible to forbid the drinking of intoxicants, so in a number of Welsh parishes rest houses, under ecclesiastical control, were established near a church, and travellers were given a fairly mild alcoholic beverage called *cwrw*, a kind of beer, not that exceptionally strong intoxicant *metheglyn* or mead, much loved by the Welsh. Even so, it is said that at Llanelltyd during the nineteenth century when the gold rush was at its height in the neighbourhood, many fights took place in front of Tyn 'y llan, the Cornish miners being among the worst offenders. But as the Temperance Movement gained strength in Wales, inns run by the Church gradually closed down and became private houses. At Llanelltyd the steps cut in the circular churchyard wall for the convenience of worshippers who wanted to get refreshment at Tyn 'y llan can still be seen.

The departure of the monks from Cymer Abbey was a spiritual disaster for Llanelltyd and the church was left without a priest until 1604. It now forms part of the rectorial benefice of Dolgellau.

Within the compass of one book it is impossible to give a complete picture of the Welsh people, but it is hoped that some idea has been given of the ancient crafts they practised, their curious customs, a few of which have not yet quite fallen into desuetude, and the strange legends, many containing a germ of truth.

Index